ART OF THE GOLD RUSH

R

ART
OF THE
GOLD RUSH

Janice T. Driesbach

Harvey L. Jones

and

Katherine Church Holland

OAKLAND MUSEUM OF CALIFORNIA

CROCKER ART MUSEUM

AND

UNIVERSITY OF CALIFORNIA PRESS

Copublished by the Oakland Museum of California, the Crocker Art Museum, and the University of California Press.

Exhibition Schedule

OAKLAND MUSEUM *of* CALIFORNIA
Oakland, California
24 January–31 May 1998

CROCKER ART MUSEUM
Sacramento, California
21 June–13 September 1998

NATIONAL MUSEUM *of* AMERICAN ART
Smithsonian Institution
Washington, D.C.
30 October 1998–7 March 1999

LIBRARY OF CONGRESS CATALOGING-IN-PUBLICATION DATA

Driesbach, Janice Tolhurst.
Art of the gold rush / by Janice T. Driesbach, Harvey L. Jones, and Katherine Church Holland.
p. cm.
Catalog of an exhibition held at the Oakland Museum of California, Oakland, Calif., Jan. 24–May 31, 1998; Crocker Art Museum, Sacramento, Calif., June 21–Sept. 13, 1998; National Museum of American Art, Smithsonian Institution, Washington, D.C., Oct. 30, 1998–Mar. 7, 1999.
Includes bibliographical references and index.
ISBN 0-520-21431-5 (cloth : alk. paper).—ISBN 0-520-21432-3 (pbk. : alk. paper)
1. Art, American—California—Exhibitions. 2. Art, Modern—19th century—California—Exhibitions. 3. Gold mines and mining in art. 4. California—Gold discoveries—Pictorial works—Exhibitions. I. Jones, Harvey L. II. Holland, Katherine Church. III. Oakland Museum. IV. Crocker Art Museum. V. National Museum of American Art (U.S.) VI. Title.
N6530.C2D75 1998 97-29319
759.194'07494—dc21 CIP

EXHIBITION CURATORS: Janice T. Driesbach and Harvey L. Jones
EDITOR: Frances Bowles
DESIGNER: Gordon Chun Design, Berkeley, California

COVER IMAGE: Charles Christian Nahl, *Sunday Morning in the Mines,* 1872, fig. 81

Printed in Italy by Graphicom Srl
9 8 7 6 5 4 3 2 1

Contents

LIST OF ILLUSTRATIONS *vii*

FOREWORD

Stephen C. McGough and Dennis M. Power *xi*

ACKNOWLEDGMENTS

Harvey L. Jones, Janice T. Driesbach, and Katherine C. Holland *xiii*

LENDERS TO THE EXHIBITION *xv*

MAP OF THE GOLD COUNTRY *xvii*

INTRODUCTION

The Lure of Gold

Janice T. Driesbach 1

FIRST IN THE FIELD

Thomas A. Ayres and E. Hall Martin

Janice T. Driesbach and Harvey L. Jones 7

SCENES OF MINING LIFE

John Prendergast, Augusto Ferran, William McIlvaine, W. Taber, William Birch McMurtrie, Harrison Eastman, Samuel Stillman Osgood, A. G., John Henry Dunnel, Washington F. Friend, John Woodhouse Audubon, Francis Samuel Marryat, and E. Godchaux

Janice T. Driesbach 15

PORTRAIT PAINTER TO THE ELITE

William Smith Jewett

Janice T. Driesbach 37

THE HESSIAN PARTY

Charles Christian Nahl, Arthur Nahl, and August Wenderoth

Harvey L. Jones 47

SOUVENIRS OF THE MOTHER LODE
Ernest Narjot and George Henry Burgess
Harvey L. Jones 65

MINING THE PICTURESQUE
A. D. O. Browere
Janice T. Driesbach 77

IN THE WAKE OF THE GOLD RUSH
Frederick A. Butman, Alexander Edouart, and George Tirrell
Janice T. Driesbach 91

SENTIMENT AND NOSTALGIA
Charles Christian Nahl, Ernest Narjot, George Henry Burgess, Henry Bacon, and Rufus Wright
Harvey L. Jones 101

BIOGRAPHIES OF THE ARTISTS
Katherine Church Holland 117

NOTES 132

SELECTED BIBLIOGRAPHY 138

LIST OF ARTISTS REPRESENTED IN THE EXHIBITION 140

INDEX 142

Illustrations

The Gold Country *(map), xvii*

Mountain Jack and a Wandering Miner, E. Hall Martin, *xviii*
California News, William Sidney Mount, 3

San Francisco Bay, Thomas A. Ayres, 6
Sunrise at Camp Lonely from the South, Looking North, Thomas A. Ayres, 7
Camp Lonely from the North . . . by Moonlight, Thomas A. Ayres, 8
Bay of San Francisco, View from Telegraph Hill Looking Toward Saucelito, Thomas A. Ayres, 9
North Beach: San Francisco from Off Meigs' Wharf, Thomas A. Ayres, 9
The Prospector, E. Hall Martin, 12
Oedipus and the Sphinx, Jean-Auguste-Dominique Ingres, 13

San Francisco after Fire, John Prendergast, 16
Album Californiano, 12. Realizacion. Selling Off, Augusto Ferran, 17
San Francisco: View from the Hills to Northwest, Augusto Ferran, 18
Vista de San Francisco, Augusto Ferran, 18
Panning Gold, California, William McIlvaine, 19
Prairie, California, William McIlvaine, 20
Steam Gold Dredger Ascending the Sacramento, W. Taber, 21
View of Telegraph Hill and City, North on Montgomery Street, William Birch McMurtrie, 22
Saint Francis Hotel, Cor. Clay and Dupont Sts., Harrison Eastman, 23
General John A. Sutter, Samuel Stillman Osgood, 24
A Lucky Striker, Artist unknown ("A.G."), 25
Placer Mining, Washington F. Friend, 26
Sutter's Mill at Coloma, John Henry Dunnel, 26
Mining Scene: Diverting a River, Artist unknown, 27
Mining in California, Artist unknown, 28
Twenty-five Miles West of Jesus Maria, John Woodhouse Audubon, 29
Murphy's New Diggings (Oak of the Hills), John Woodhouse Audubon, 30
Hawkin's Bar, John Woodhouse Audubon, 31
Sacramento City, John Woodhouse Audubon, 31
San Francisco, John Woodhouse Audubon, 32
San Francisco Fire of 17 September 1850, Francis Samuel Marryat, 34
Vue de San-Francisco en 1851, E. Godchaux, 35

Captain Washington A. Bartlett, U.S.N., William Smith Jewett, 36
The Promised Land—The Grayson Family, William Smith Jewett, 39
Hock Farm (A View of the Butte Mountains from Feather River, California), William Smith Jewett, 41
Hock Farm, William Smith Jewett, 41
Captain Ned Wakeman, William Smith Jewett, 42
Portrait of General John A. Sutter, William Smith Jewett, 43
Portrait of General John A. Sutter, William Smith Jewett, 45
Yosemite Falls, William Smith Jewett, 46
Pursued, William Smith Jewett, 46

Portrait of a Man, Frederick August Wenderoth, 48
Saturday Night at the Mines, Charles Christian Nahl and Hugo Wilhelm Arthur Nahl, 49
Miners in the Sierra, Charles Christian Nahl and Frederick August Wenderoth, 50
The Fire in Sacramento, Hugo Wilhelm Arthur Nahl, 52
The Camp of a U.S. Coast Geodetic Survey Party, Charles Christian Nahl and Hugo Wilhelm Arthur Nahl, 53
Fire in San Francisco Bay, Charles Christian Nahl and Hugo Wilhelm Arthur Nahl, 55
Chagres River Scene (Crossing the Chagres), Charles Christian Nahl, 57
Boaters Rowing to Shore at Chagres, Charles Christian Nahl, 58
Little Miss San Francisco, Charles Christian Nahl, 59
Portrait of Jane Eliza Steen Johnson, Charles Christian Nahl, 60
Madame Moitessier, Jean-Auguste-Dominique Ingres, 61
Fandango, Charles Christian Nahl, 63

Placer Operations at Foster's Bar, Ernest Narjot, 64
Hunters in the Gold Country, George Henry Burgess, 67
Untitled (man crossing a stream), George Henry Burgess, 68
Miners Working Beside a Stream, George Henry Burgess, 68
Artist's Gold Mining Camp, George Henry Burgess, 69
Mining at Tunnel Hill, Jackson, Amador County, California, George Henry Burgess, 71
Mother Lode Inn, George Henry Burgess, 71
San Francisco in July, 1849, George Henry Burgess, 73

The Lone Prospector, A. D. O. Browere, 76
Catskill, New York, A. D. O. Browere, 77
Miner's Return, A. D. O. Browere, 78
John C. Duchow, Jr., A. D. O. Browere, 80
Miners of Placerville, A. D. O. Browere, 81
Prospectors in the Sierra, A. D. O. Browere, 82
Jamestown or D. O. Mills' Mill, A. D. O. Browere, 83
Stockton, A. D. O. Browere, 85
View of Stockton, A. D. O. Browere, 85
Mokelumne Hill, A. D. O. Browere, 86
The Trail of the '49ers, A. D. O. Browere, 87
The Voyage of Life: Youth, Thomas Cole, 87
Crossing the Isthmus, A. D. O. Browere, 88
Goldminers, A. D. O. Browere, 89
South of Tuolumne City, A. D. O. Browere, 89

Surveyor's Camp, Frederick Butman, 92
Hunter's Point, Frederick Butman, 94
Chinese Fishing Village, Frederick Butman, 95
Blessing of the Enrequita Mine, Alexander Edouart, 97
View of Sacramento, California, from Across the Sacramento River, George Tirrell, 99

Sunday Morning in the Mines, Charles Christian Nahl, 100
Dead Miner, Charles Christian Nahl, 103
Forest Burial, attributed to Charles Christian Nahl, 104
The Forty-Niner, Ernest Narjot, 106
Miners: A Moment at Rest (Gold Rush Camp), Ernest Narjot, 107
French Gold-Seekers in California, Ernest Narjot, 109
View of San Francisco in 1850, George Henry Burgess, 111
The Luck of Roaring Camp, Oscar Kunath, 112
The Luck of Roaring Camp, Henry Bacon, 113
The Card Players, Rufus Wright, 115

Foreword

As the sesquicentennial of the discovery of gold in California approaches, it is particularly appropriate that our two California-focused institutions collaborate on an exhibition that presents and interprets the rich legacy of painting created during and about the Gold Rush.

The first public museum in continuous existence west of the Mississippi River, the Crocker Art Museum was founded by citizens lured west by California's mineral wealth and rapid growth. Following financial success realized from the construction of the transcontinental railroad, itself hastened by the discovery of gold, Edwin Bryant Crocker and his wife, Margaret, began acquiring master paintings and drawings in Europe. They also purchased many outstanding examples created by artists working in Northern California during the early 1870s, a time when the local art community—with its origins in the Gold Rush—had matured to become a major regional arts center, boasting an art association, numerous exhibition opportunities, and a school of design. Among Crocker's perceptive acquisitions was his commission in 1872 of Charles Christian Nahl's *Sunday Morning in the Mines,* a potent moral allegory that came to embody the Gold Rush in the minds of many, despite having been created two decades after the events depicted. The many paintings by Nahl and other early California artists—among them, Norton Bush, Thomas Hill, and William Keith—purchased by the Crockers established a collecting focus for the museum that has since been strengthened by important additions.

The Oakland Art Gallery, founded in 1916, combined with two other museums to become the Oakland Museum of California. Since 1969, the museum has charted a distinctive course in its focus on the art, history, and natural science of California. In addressing this rich regional heritage, visionary leaders brought together an impressive collection of California art that includes strong holdings by many of the artists active during and following the Gold Rush. In the museum's collections are paintings that superbly document the range of well-known artists such as William Smith Jewett and the Nahl brothers, as well as rare examples by largely undiscovered talents, such as E. Hall Martin and John Prendergast.

These resources offer an excellent opportunity to study the art of the Gold Rush, which, despite pioneering publications by Jeanne Van Nostrand, Dr. Joseph A. Baird Jr., and others, remains a largely overlooked era in American art. The accomplishments of the Hudson River school, the early genre painters in the East and Midwest, and the realist artists who emerged after the Civil War have been widely studied, but the contemporaneous painted record of California's early notables, culture, and landscape has not been similarly explored. As with other events precipitated by James Marshall's discovery of gold in the American River east of Sacramento in January 1848, developments in the art of California had an influence beyond the geographic limits of the goldfields and the surrounding communities at that time and for decades thereafter. *Art of the Gold Rush* seeks to share both the quality and diversity of this artistic record, and to explore its contributions in documenting and interpreting this fascinating period.

We would like to recognize the work of the curators, Janice T. Driesbach of the Crocker Art Museum and Harvey L. Jones of the Oakland Museum of California, for their partnership in organizing this exhibition and writing this book, to which Katherine Church Holland has made a splendid contribution in writing the biographies of the artists. Their research has been assisted by the generosity of other private collectors and public institutions in Northern California. The Bancroft Library of the University of California, Berkeley, and the California Historical Society, in particular, offered critical support to *Art of the Gold Rush* by making significant loans to the exhibition and providing extensive research assistance. Katherine Holland, formerly at the California Historical Society, and Charles Faulhaber, director, and William Roberts of the Bancroft Library were instrumental to the realization of the exhibition and its accompanying publication. *Art of the Gold Rush* has been greatly enriched by the support of numerous lenders, whose enthusiasm and willingness to share from their collections have made this exhibition and its tour possible.

Presenting sponsors for the *Art of the Gold Rush* exhibition and book are the Oakland Museum Women's Board, the Crocker Art Museum Association, the California Arts Council, Christie's, the Clorox Company Foundation, and others who prefer to remain anonymous. Major sponsors include the Barkley Fund, the Walter and Elise Haas Fund, Wells Fargo, the S. H. Cowell Foundation, the Levi Strauss Foundation, the City of Sacramento, The Bernard Osher Foundation, Pacific Gas and Electric Company, the Rockefeller Foundation, and the L. J. Skaggs and Mary C. Skaggs Foundation. Contributing sponsors are the Richard and Rhoda Goldman Fund, Mr. and Mrs. Ellis Stephens, Union Bank of California, David and Lyn Anderson, Crosby Heafey Roach & May, Helen F. Novy, Albert Shumate, William F. Weeden, and other members and friends of the Oakland Museum of California.

Stephen C. McGough
Director, Crocker Art Museum

Dennis M. Power
Executive Director, Oakland Museum of California

Acknowledgments

As authors of *Art of the Gold Rush*, we wish to acknowledge the many individuals and institutions who have so generously contributed to both the exhibition and this book. We thank those who have helped our organization of the exhibition by directing us to paintings that we might otherwise not have known or found: Marjorie C. Arkelian, Eric Baumgartner, John H. Garzoli, Alfred C. Harrison Jr., Mark Hoffman, and Nan and Roy Farrington Jones.

We owe a debt of thanks to colleagues at several institutions who provided information about the art and artists represented in the exhibition: James E. Henley, Director, Sacramento Archives and Museum Collection Center; Patricia Keats, Director of the Library, and Bo Mompho, Curatorial Assistant, at the California Historical Society; Gary Kurutz and the staff of the California State Library; Charlene Noyes, Archivist, Sacramento Archives and Museum Collection Center; William Roberts, Acting Curator, Pictorial Collections, the Bancroft Library, University of California, Berkeley; and Kim Walters, Librarian, Southwest Museum.

We are grateful to friends and colleagues whose encouragement and support have advanced the project in many ways: Elizabeth Broun, Merry Foresta, George Gurney, Therese Thau Heyman, Charles J. Robertson, and Kenneth R. Trapp at the National Museum of American Art, Smithsonian Institution; and Kevin Starr, Librarian of the California State Library.

Special thanks to Frances Bowles for her patience, insight, and good humor as editor of the manuscript and for her careful attention to the preparation of all the text. We are indebted, also, to Kathy Borgogno for her assistance in many aspects of the project, to Lorene Anderson for her help in securing the images and information for the captions for the illustrations, and to Janet Correia for her help.

Essential to the project were the contributions of several members of the staff of the Crocker Art Museum: Paulette Hennum, Registrar; Karen Hulett Brown, Curatorial Assistant; KD Kurutz, Curator of Education; Patrick Minor and Steve Wilson, Exhibit Coordinators. Our appreciation extends to staff members of the Oakland Museum of California whose contributions were key to the project: Philip Linhares, Chief Curator of Art; Drew Johnson, Associate Curator of Photography; Arthur Monroe, Registrar; Gianna Capecci, Registrar; Karen Nelson, Interpretive Specialist; Joy Tehan, Assistant Registrar; David Ruddell, Exhibit Preparator; Brian Wheeler, Technical Specialist; Inez Brooks-Myers, Associate Curator of History; Tom Steller, Interim Chief Curator of Natural Science; and Cherie Newell, Historical Researcher.

We gratefully acknowledge the Co-Trustees of the Crocker Art Museum and the Trustees of the Oakland Museum of California Foundation for their sustained interest in this auspicious joint project.

For their encouragement and support in the production of the book, our appreciation goes to Deborah Kirshman, Marilyn Schwartz, and Anthony Crouch at the University of California Press.

Special thanks to Gordon Chun of Gordon Chun Design for the sensitive and attractive design and layout of the book.

Harvey L. Jones
Janice T. Driesbach
Katherine C. Holland

Lenders to the Exhibition

Achenbach Foundation for Graphic Arts, the Fine Arts Museums of San Francisco
Autry Museum of Western Heritage, Los Angeles
The Bancroft Library, University of California, Berkeley
California Historical Society, San Francisco
Louis A. Capellino
Crocker Art Museum, Sacramento
M. H. de Young Memorial Museum, the Fine Arts Museums of San Francisco
Garzoli Gallery, San Rafael, California
The Gilcrease Museum, Tulsa, Oklahoma
Eldon and Susan Grupp
F. E. Keeler III
Dr. Oscar and Trudy Lemer
James and Susan McClatchy
Everett Millard
Museum of Fine Arts, Boston
The National Cowboy Hall of Fame and Western Heritage Center, Oklahoma City, Oklahoma
National Museum of American Art, Smithsonian Institution, Washington, D.C.
Oakland Museum of California
Hideko Goto Packard
Mr. and Mrs. A. R. Phillips Jr.
Post Road Gallery, Larchmont, New York
Private collections
Sacramento Archives and Museum Collection Center
Santa Barbara Historical Society
Santa Barbara Museum of Art
Southwest Museum, Los Angeles

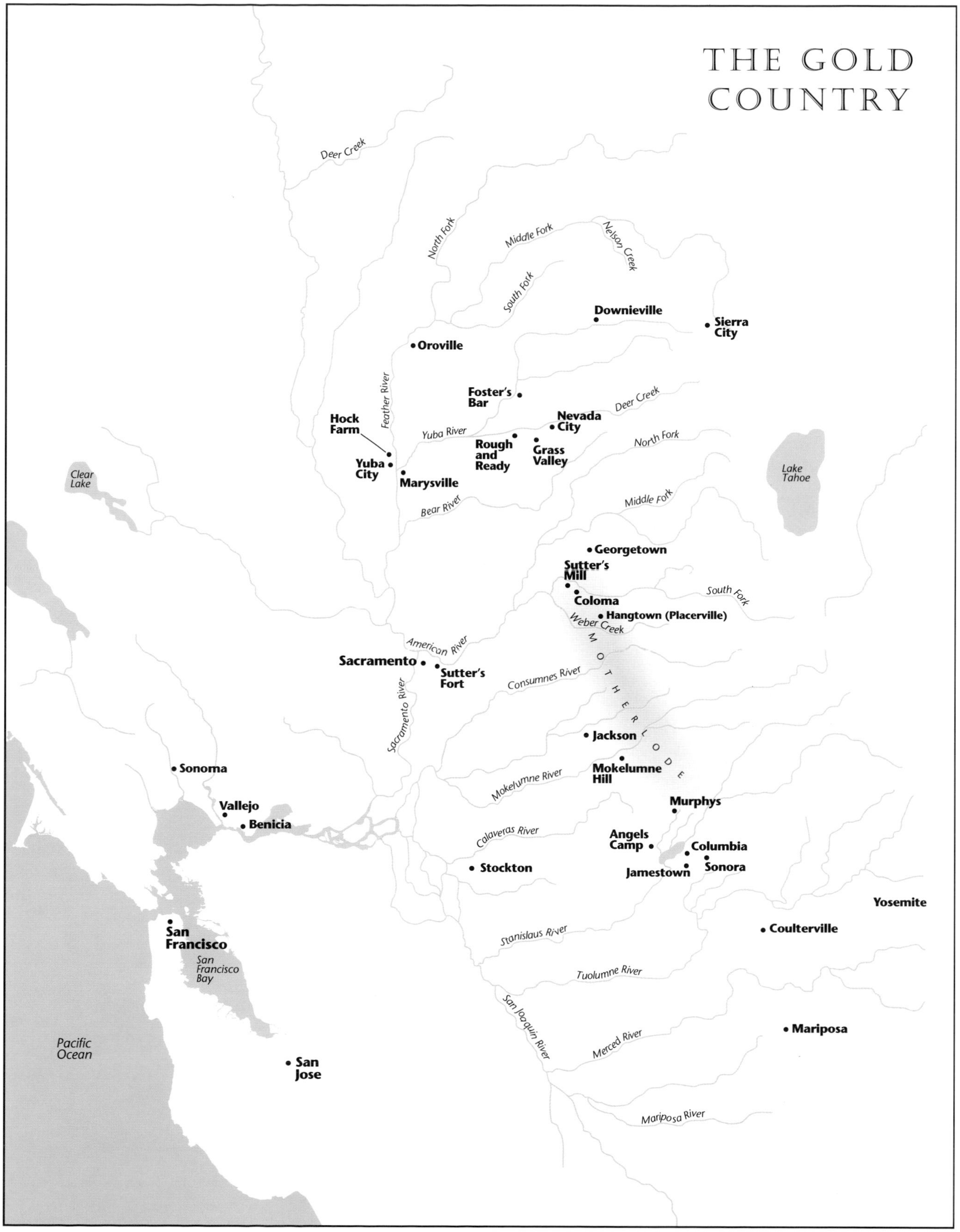
THE GOLD COUNTRY
Deer Creek
North Fork
Middle Fork
Nelson Creek
South Fork
Downieville
Sierra City
Oroville
Feather River
Foster's Bar
Deer Creek
Nevada City
Hock Farm
Yuba River
Rough and Ready
Grass Valley
North Fork
Yuba City
Marysville
Lake Tahoe
Clear Lake
Bear River
Middle Fork
Georgetown
Sutter's Mill
Coloma
South Fork
Hangtown (Placerville)
Weber Creek
MOTHER LODE
American River
Sacramento
Sutter's Fort
Consumnes River
Sacramento River
Jackson
Sonoma
Mokelumne River
Mokelumne Hill
Vallejo
Benicia
Murphys
Calaveras River
Angels Camp
Columbia
Stockton
Jamestown
Sonora
Yosemite
Coulterville
San Francisco
Stanislaus River
San Francisco Bay
Tuolumne River
San Joaquin River
Mariposa
Pacific Ocean
Merced River
San Jose
Mariposa River

FIG. 1. E. Hall Martin, *Mountain Jack and a Wandering Miner,* 1850. Oil on canvas, 39½ × 72 in. Oakland Museum of California, gift of Concours d'Antiques, Art Guild.

Introduction

THE LURE OF GOLD

Janice T. Driesbach

James Marshall's discovery of gold along the American River near Sacramento in January 1848 precipitated an influx of immigrants from all over the world to California in search of promised wealth. Rumors of gold began circulating soon after Marshall took his find to John Sutter at Sutter's Fort, where the two confirmed, to the best of their knowledge, that the metal was indeed gold. Sutter tried to keep the discovery secret, but word soon traveled, carried by teamsters delivering goods to Coloma, among others. Although announcements appeared in San Francisco papers by mid-March, it was not until 12 May, when Samuel Brannan—who operated a store at Sutter's Fort—arrived in San Francisco, a bag of gold dust in hand and shouting: "Gold! Gold! Gold from the American River!" that workers abandoned their jobs to head for the Sierra foothills.[1] When ore samples reached Monterey the following month, "the blacksmith dropped his hammer, the carpenter his plane, the mason his trowel, the baker his loaf, and the tapster his bottle."[2] Gold fever spread quickly, first to towns throughout California. Soon immigrants from Mexico and Chile, pioneers who had traveled west to Oregon, and local Native Americans were all prospecting along streams traversing the Sierra Nevada from the Yuba River in the north to the Mokelumne in the southern Sierra.[3] On the East Coast of the United States the first reports were received with skepticism and a suspicion that the so-called discovery was a ruse to entice American settlers to isolated outposts in the Far West.[4]

Less than two weeks after Marshall spotted gold in his millrace, Mexico transferred vast holdings in the Southwest, including all of California, to the United States by the Treaty of Guadalupe Hidalgo. At the time, Spanish-speaking Californios accounted for half or more of the estimated ten thousand people, excluding Native Americans, residing in the area. Among the rest were recent American immigrants and Russian and British traders and trappers.[5]

By the fall of 1848, reports and samples of the gold submitted by Governor Richard Mason and Lieutenant Edward F. Beale reached Washington. With this evidence, President James K. Polk announced the discovery in his annual address to Congress, stimulating thousands of Americans to make plans to set out to seek their fortunes.[6] Whether by sea (at first around Cape Horn, and later across the Isthmus of Panama) or overland (after spring snowmelt so stock could feed on grass and before winter storms made the Sierra impassable), the arduous journeys demanded considerable energy and expense. Most travel would take five or six months, and would-be miners—of diverse ages, but overwhelmingly male—frequently had to borrow money from friends and family, forming investment companies to underwrite their enterprise. Nonetheless, most of the Argonauts—a name adopted by the miners and their contemporaries in acknowledgment of the adventure they were undertaking—saw themselves as sojourners in California, intending to reap their rewards quickly and return home.

Overland travel terminated at Sierra mining sites. From about mid-1849 on, ships carrying gold-seekers from the East Coast arrived en masse in San Francisco harbor. They joined vessels from Europe, where accounts of the gold discovery were received amidst food shortages and widespread political turmoil. Aspiring miners were coming from as far away as Australia and China, acquiring essential supplies—often at exorbitant prices—and heading to the mines, weather permitting. By the end of 1849, as a result of this unprecedented international migration, California's population had swelled tenfold.[7]

Before the Gold Rush, settlers from the East and Midwest—where the Swiss-born Sutter had stopped as well—had been arriving in California for some time, but the challenges of the overland trek and Mexico's refusal to allow noncitizens to hold title to property had kept their numbers small. Nonetheless, by 1846, there was a growing American and European presence in California; Sutter could envision establishing a community, to be called Sutterville, close to the fort he commanded near the confluence of the Sacramento and American rivers, on property granted him by the Mexican government in 1839. In August 1847 he contracted with James Marshall to build a sawmill at Coloma.[8]

Despite increasing immigration and intrigues between Mexican and American political factions, there is scant visual record of California in the months preceding the gold discovery.[9] With the arrival of the Argonauts, however, an outpouring of watercolors, drawings, and ambitious oil paintings documented and interpreted the Gold Rush locales, participants, and activities. Unlike earlier immigrants—and previous waves of settlement in the United States spearheaded by would-be farmers—miners flocking to California generally came without their families and were trained in diverse occupations; among them were artists and writers, merchants, machinists, shoemakers, and silversmiths.[10] That many sought to bring some aspects of the cultivated surroundings they had left behind into their new lives is reflected in accounts that describe musical ensembles formed at sea by miners who brought their instruments with them, and the popularity of traveling theater troupes in Gold Rush communities large and small.[11] The miners' awareness that they were participating in a historical event and the exotic character of their undertaking stimulated them to record both the everyday and the exceptional events they encountered. Enforced inactivity, when winter rains precluded mining, may also have encouraged their artistic pursuits.

Few views of the Gold Rush were produced by established East Coast artists of the day (William

Sidney Mount's *California News* [fig. 2] is a notable exception), but a number of capable painters traveled west. Many were lured to California—as were their colleagues—expecting success in the diggings, and returned to their original occupations only when wealth in the placers eluded them. Other painters and illustrators embarked for California for different reasons: the adventure itself, a desire to make money by publishing accounts or creating panoramas for audiences in Europe or the East, or to pursue careers in new communities that had fewer restrictions and less competition. Whatever their motives in joining the California Gold Rush, the painters and draftsmen (some with the advantage of art school training, and others apparently self-taught) created engrossing images of the scenery, people, and activities around them. The results were often satisfying accomplishments of artistic merit, as well as compelling, firsthand documents of their remarkable ventures. In images ranging from casually rendered drawings of mining-camp scenes to large oil paintings commissioned by patrons, artists such as William Smith Jewett, Charles Christian Nahl, A. D. O. Browere, and others created a visual legacy of the Gold Rush. Their images were important in providing information about California and life at the time and in crafting representations of local notables. The paintings and drawings were exhibited in the East and translated into lithographs for international distribution. Along with written accounts—including letters and journals—and daguerreotypes, their efforts afford viewers today a significant understanding of the natural resources, economic changes, and cultural development that distinguished the Gold Rush in California. *Art of the Gold Rush* explores only part of that vast visual legacy. The focus of the exhibition—and thus of this book—is on original works of art, selected because they represent particular themes and for their high artistic quality.

FIG. 2. William Sidney Mount, *California News,* 1850. Oil on canvas, 21½ × 20¼ in. Museums at Stony Brook, New York, gift of Mr. and Mrs. Ward Melville.

Like other American art of this period, images of the Gold Rush were created almost exclusively by men of European descent who brought their perceptions and the technical conventions in which they were trained (generally in the East or Europe) to their representations of new subjects. What they chose to depict and how their motifs were presented embody the cultural biases of a subset of the thousands of people from throughout the world who participated in the event. Only a small percentage of the paintings, watercolors, and drawings created during this remarkable time survives today. Fires that swept through San Francisco (including the devastating blaze that followed the earthquake in 1906) destroyed many works; others were lost to various natural calamities or to carelessness. Examples of Gold Rush painting are therefore rare and prized, and only incompletely document the exceptional outpouring of artwork that characterized this period. Nonetheless, the art of the Gold Rush contributes significantly to our understanding of both American culture and its interpreters during the third quarter of the nineteenth century.

What we have documents rapidly changing events that had an ongoing impact on California. Even in the initial months of mining, conditions and technologies changed dramatically. We can date drawings and paintings with some certainty from depictions of mining tools or the types of operations. Artists arrived in successive waves and made their way to the mines by various routes. When passage across Panama via the Chagres River gained popularity over the trip around the Horn, for instance, representations of Panama's verdant tropical landscape become abundant. Nostalgia for the recent past set in quite early. By the mid-1850s, artists such as A. D. O. Browere were producing romanticized paintings that showed earlier—rather than current—Gold Rush practices (see figs. 65 and 74). Artists also responded to an evolving audience for their work. Most of their earliest productions were realized as prints or illustrations, but by 1850 large oil paintings, such as E. Hall Martin's *Mountain Jack and a Wandering Miner* (fig. 1) or William Smith Jewett's *The Promised Land* (fig. 33) were also in demand. Little information survives about art patronage of this period, but it is clear that changes were taking place. And, although the Gold Rush is considered to have spent itself by 1854, artists continued to arrive in California, to explore both the possibilities of mining and the state's other attractions.

Contrary to the perception that portraits dominated early Gold Rush art, scenes of developing cities and mining sites are well represented in drawings and watercolors in 1849 and early 1850 (see Augusto Ferran's *Vista de San Francisco* [fig. 13] and Harrison Eastman's watercolor *Saint Francis Hotel* [fig. 18]). Late in 1849, one of the earliest known public displays of artwork in San Francisco consisted of scenes sketched "in all parts of California" by William Cogswell, who planned "to take these to the eastern states to show graphically and truly California scenes, men, and women."[12] Landscape figures prominently in William McIlvaine's sumptuous watercolors (figs. 14 and 15), although they also contain elements of genre painting—scenes of everyday life—in their depiction of mining and camp life.

There was a growing taste for genre painting among the American public by midcentury, and Argonauts engaged in mining tasks assume prominent roles in some of the large canvases being produced at this time, among them Martin's images of prospectors, and in scenes such as *The Lone Prospector* by A. D. O. Browere (fig. 61). The ambitious scope of such compositions suggests that, although San Francisco boasted few artistic resources in the early 1850s (Benjamin Parke Avery noted that few examples of European painting were available),[13] patronage was growing and a community of artists was beginning to develop.

Nonetheless, the *First Industrial Exhibition of the Mechanics' Institute* in 1857 was the initial opportunity afforded to artists in San Francisco to show their work to the public—and view the accomplishments of their colleagues—on a large scale. The dominance of portraiture among the offerings was duly noted in the catalogue, with the statement that "the luxuries of painting can only follow the introduction of wealth-creating improvements, and it cannot be expected at this epoch of development of arts in California that the talents of artists in this class will be duly encouraged."[14] Within a few years, however, several artists of stature were attracted by the state's magnificent landscape and moderate climate, as well as by the prosperity that followed in the wake of the Gold Rush. By 1863, when Samuel Marsden Brookes, Thomas Hill, and Virgil Williams were among the resident artists, and Albert Bierstadt first visited the state, John S. Hittell could make the following assessment:

> Art does not flourish usually in new countries. The proportion of rich families is small; and most of the rich, having become suddenly wealthy, are unaccustomed to frequent contemplation of fine pictures, have not taste, and perhaps cover their walls with miserable daubs. We could not expect therefore that art would more than exist in California, . . . But it does exist.[15]

Artists participated in the Gold Rush in various ways. Some arrived in California, proceeded to travel through the mining communities, responding to the views and activities they witnessed, and soon returned home. Some, such as Martin and Thomas A. Ayres, succumbed to the diseases or dangers that cut short the lives of many Forty-niners. Others established studios in Sacramento or San Francisco, found markets for their work, and became long-term residents who contributed to the development of Northern California as a major regional art center later in the century.

FIG. 3. Thomas A. Ayres, *San Francisco Bay,* 1851. Watercolor, gouache, and pencil on paper, 6¾ × 6¾ in. Oakland Museum of California, gift of the Reichel Fund.

First in the Field

THOMAS A. AYRES AND E. HALL MARTIN

Janice T. Driesbach and Harvey L. Jones

AMONG THE FIRST ARTISTS BOOKING PASSAGE to California from the East following news of the gold discovery were Thomas A. Ayres and E. Hall Martin. Both boarded the *Panama* in New Jersey on 4 February 1849 and arrived in San Francisco in early August. There is no evidence Ayres and Martin knew each other previously, but they surely became acquainted during the long passage. Although they were contemporaries and both had careers as artists, Ayres as a draftsman with an engineering firm in St. Paul, Minnesota, and Martin as a painter in Cincinnati, they do not appear to have stayed in contact after reaching San Francisco.

There is little information on Ayres's activities in the months following his arrival in California. He probably proceeded to the mines, and—like other artist Argonauts—in due course returned to the profession in which he was trained. It is likely that Ayres made his two views of Camp Lonely while wandering through northern California transcribing scenery. Because they are more primitive than many of his works and show the quiet river views more characteristic of the early months of mining, these may be among his first black chalk drawings of California. Like many of the artist's drawings, they are on coarsely textured board that resembles sandpaper. This surface is easily abraded, and *Camp Lonely from the North . . . by Moonlight* (fig. 5) and *Sunrise at Camp Lonely from the South, Looking North* (fig. 4) are scratched. Both compositions show a foreground river flanked by nearly vertical hillsides sparsely dotted with pine trees. The minuscule figure and tent in *Sunrise at Camp Lonely* make the mountains seem even more mammoth. Ayres's use of monochromatic gray tones reinforces the sense of isolation and suggests how the spot received its name.

Fig. 4. Thomas A. Ayres, *Sunrise at Camp Lonely from the South, Looking North,* ca. 1850. Black chalk on sand-coated paper, 7½ × 10⅜ in. The Bancroft Library, University of California, Berkeley.

Although Ayres is best known for his black-and-white drawings, *San Francisco Bay* (fig. 3), of 1851, demonstrates his abilities as a colorist. Painted in gouache (or opaque watercolor) and watercolor over a pencil sketch on tan paper, this small study shows the artist's command of detail in its depiction of a number of boats on the bay.

Masts and rigging are carefully described, even on the background vessels, and deft touches of color enliven the scene.

By 1854, Ayres had embarked on an ambitious project to have forty-six of his drawings translated as oil paintings for exhibition as a "Panorama of California." Perhaps seeking to capitalize on the popularity of huge panoramas of western landscape subjects, Ayres commissioned Thomas A. Smith to make the oil paintings (now lost) after his drawings of the mining regions. Their subjects indicate that the artist journeyed to mining camps from Mount Shasta in the north through Coloma, Placerville, and Tuolumne to Tejon Pass (where he recorded a Native American encampment) in the south during his travels. Although most of his views were landscapes, the titles suggest that Ayres occasionally depicted miners at work (in Nevada City and at Murderer's Bar), as well as exotic activities such as "Lassoing Wild Horses" in the Tulare Valley. In the flyer he published to accompany the "Panorama of California," Ayres declared the pictures were "painted expressly for exhibition in the Atlantic states and in Europe," to contribute to "the already high character of California abroad."[1] Before taking the panorama east, however, Ayres exhibited the paintings at both D. L. Gunn's art store and at Musical Hall in San Francisco, where they were enthusiastically received.[2]

FIG. 5. Thomas A. Ayres, *Camp Lonely from the North . . . by Moonlight,* ca. 1850. Black chalk on sand-coated paper, 7½ × 10⅜ in. The Bancroft Library, University of California, Berkeley.

Bay of San Francisco, View of Telegraph Hill Looking Toward Saucelito (fig. 6) may be a study for a panorama painting of the same title. This idyllic view is one of several drawings of San Francisco Bay that Ayres made in 1854 and 1855, and may also have been intended as a model for a lithograph.[3] In its view past Alcatraz Island, the composition is nearly identical with that of another drawing Ayres completed the following year. The buildings lining the bay and Meiggs' Wharf jutting into the harbor testify to San Francisco's steady growth following the Gold Rush. The family group atop Telegraph Hill also documents that the city was becoming a settled community.

North Beach: San Francisco from Off Meigs' Wharf (fig. 7), offers a view from the opposite direction, looking south toward the city. The three boats in the foreground—clipper ship, sailboat, and steamer—represent different types of vessels that plied San Francisco Bay, and each reappears in other contemporary drawings by Ayres. Meiggs' Wharf in the distance and the houses scattered in the background (as well as the telegraph station on the hill) show how San Francisco has grown.[4] These polished drawings

FIG. 6. Thomas A. Ayres, *Bay of San Francisco, View from Telegraph Hill Looking Toward Saucelito,* 1854. Graphite, charcoal, opaque watercolor, and scratching on sand-coated paper mounted on card, 12⅞ × 22⅞ in. Fine Arts Museums of San Francisco, Achenbach Foundation for Graphic Arts, gift of Miss T. Throckmorton in memory of Robert E. Throckmorton. 41052

FIG. 7. Thomas A. Ayres, *North Beach: San Francisco from Off Meigs' Wharf,* 1854. Graphite, charcoal, opaque watercolor, and scratching on sand-coated paper mounted on card, 12⅞ × 22⅞ in. Fine Arts Museums of San Francisco, Achenbach Foundation for Graphic Arts, gift of Miss T. Throckmorton in memory of Robert E. Throckmorton. 41051.

also document Ayres's growing abilities as an artist, now able to compose successful large-scale views that offer considerable detail. Again Ayres chose to make his drawings on commercially available paper coated with sand.[5] He continued to favor this surface, perhaps because it allowed him to create highlights by scratching through the charcoal as well as by applying opaque white pigment.

In June 1855, Thomas Ayres made history as a member of the first tourist party into Yosemite Valley. The group, assembled by James Mason Hutchings, was led by two Native American guides along an old trail from Mariposa. Ayres was invited along to make drawings for the journal Hutchings was planning—*Hutchings' Illustrated California Magazine*—and recorded some thirteen views during the five-day visit.[6] He exhibited these first drawings of Yosemite Valley at McNulty's Hall in Sacramento upon his return, and revisited Yosemite the following year to make additional drawings of the spectacular landscape. Ayres retained the second group of views, and took them with him when he traveled east in 1857. When Ayres exhibited the Yosemite drawings at the American Art Union in New York, he received "more orders than he could fill to re-produce them," as well as a commission from *Harper's Weekly* to create California views to illustrate future articles.[7] For that assignment, Ayres traveled through southern California in early 1858, embarking on a schooner at San Pedro for a return visit to San Francisco. Encountering a severe storm at sea, the ship sank soon after leaving port.

Although his career was cut short, Ayres was instrumental in developing views of California scenery in his black-and-white drawings. Ayres is best known for his views of Yosemite, which were surely critical to attracting other artists to Yosemite Valley by the late 1850s. He is, however, also distinguished as one of the first to represent the topography of the Sierra foothills (and other mining sites) and to interpret the changes San Francisco was undergoing for audiences near and far.

Faring less well than Ayres was his shipmate aboard the *Panama,* E. Hall Martin,[8] an artist of great promise, whose expectations of wealth and adventure in California soon turned to bitter disappointment and an early death. Were it not for the artistic value and Gold Rush significance attached to his only two surviving paintings, it is unlikely that Martin would be remembered at all. *Mountain Jack and a Wandering Miner* (fig. 1) and one of two companion pieces, *The Prospector* (fig. 8), are all that have been located to date. The third painting of the trilogy, with Mountain Jack as its subject, is lost.

It has been assumed that Martin was self-taught because nothing is known about his art training. The two works reveal his sophisticated painting technique, an appropriate use of atmospheric perspective, and an academic approach to figural composition that suggests that Martin had a keen awareness of European classical painting—whatever the source. Born into a poor family in Cincinnati, Ohio, Martin began painting in 1831 at the age of thirteen,[9] and was listed as a professional portrait painter in the first annual *Cincinnati Directory* for 1846 and as an artist in the New York City directory in 1847 and 1848.[10]

Although the sparse biographical information on Martin includes an unconfirmed reference to his military service in the Mexican War, there is no other evidence of any visits to Mexico before 1847, when he exhibited a painting on a Mexican subject. Titled *Castle of San Juan d'Ulloa* (the castle is at the entrance to the harbor of Veracruz, Mexico), the painting was in the 1847 exhibition of the American Academy of Fine Arts and American Art Union, along with two other works, *Boy Fishing* and *Marine View,* in 1848.[11] Another painting of a marine subject is entered into the "Record of the Western Art Union, 1849" as *Wreck of the U.S. Brig Somers.* According to information from the United States Department of the Navy, the *Somers* was engaged in blockade duty off Veracruz when it capsized and was lost in a sudden squall on 10 December 1846.[12]

Martin's participation in these annual exhibitions in New York invites speculation about his affiliation with the American Academy of Fine Arts and the American Art Union—and the possibility of his receiving some academic training while in New York. However, it also leaves little doubt about Martin's probable exposure to important American and European art being shown in New York at the time.

Leaving New York in February, Martin arrived in San Francisco on 8 August 1849. Five months later, in poor health from some undisclosed and prolonged malady that affected his ability to establish himself as an artist, he advertised his services in San Francisco's *Alta California* newspaper: "E. H. Martin, Artist, 4th St., South Side, Between Walnut and Vine." Harrison Eastman, a prominent San Francisco artist and engraver, prepared the brief advertisement, which was accompanied by a line illustration of a woman's portrait on an easel. A few days later the *Alta California* reported:

> Portrait Painter: H. Martin, artist, takes pleasure of informing the public that he has established a studio in the Haley House, upstairs, where he will be happy to paint portraits, make sketches in oil of a local character, paint landscapes or anything else in the line of his vocation. Mr. M. would invite inspection of the productions of his pencil now on hand.[13]

None of Martin's artwork from his San Francisco period has been found.

E. Hall Martin moved to Sacramento in the summer of 1850 in hopes that it would benefit his health. He accepted odd jobs, set up a studio where he secured a little patronage for his art, and began working on an allegorical trilogy of paintings with depictions of two Gold Rush characters identified as Mountain Jack and a Prospector. The first reference to any of these works comes from an editorial published 1 September 1850 in the *Illustrated California News:* "Let us mention that, among other works of art, we have been especially pleased with some very spirited and characteristic sketches in the studio of

FIG. 8. E. Hall Martin, *The Prospector,* 1850. Oil on canvas, 36 × 25 in. Mr. and Mrs. A. R. Phillips Jr.

Mr. Martin at Sacramento City, one of which, 'a Miner Prospecting,' we shall request permission to reproduce in these columns."[14] We can assume that those sketches were preparatory to the painting titled *The Prospector* (fig. 8)—and possibly the first of the three companion paintings.

The Prospector may be the earliest archetypal depiction of a Forty-niner to be found in American art, a romantic formal portrait of a Gold Rush prospector in characteristic costume: a well-worn blue shirt, patched pants, high leather boots, and a battered, wide-brimmed hat, his backpack of cooking utensils and miner's paraphernalia depicted with knowing detail. The tall, lean, bearded figure of the miner is posed standing on a mountaintop, his left foot resting on a rock. Poised between his present burden of labor and the future promise of prosperity, the prospector leans forward, with his folded arms propped up on the end of his rifle barrel, as he gazes into the distant landscape. The stance of the figure evokes classical associations with its fascinating parallel to the well-known painting *Oedipus and the Sphinx* (fig. 9) by Jean-Auguste-Dominique Ingres. The aptness of the comparison extends to the similarity in each artist's device of painting a date and his signature on a rock beneath the foot of the depicted figure. Martin's composition, color palette, and painting technique clearly reflect a sophisticated awareness of the theories and conventions of academic art.

FIG. 9. Jean-Auguste-Dominique Ingres, *Oedipus and the Sphinx,* 1808. Oil on canvas, 57¾ × 39½ in. Musée du Louvre, Paris. Photo RMN. R. G. Ojeda. 94DN60189

The painting has an interesting history that carried it beyond California after the artist's death. The clipper ship *Invincible* made its maiden voyage from the eastern United States to San Francisco, where the master, Captain Johnson, saw the painting and acquired it on behalf of a well-known American art collector in Buffalo named A. Reynolds. The painting was installed in the ship's main salon during its return trip via China and the Cape of Good Hope at the tip of Africa.[15]

In Martin's central work of the Forty-niner trilogy, *Mountain Jack and a Wandering Miner* (fig. 1), painted on a mural-sized canvas, he successfully met the aesthetic challenge of composing a scene within an unconventional, wide oval format. The landscape elements, represented by rock formations and clouds, are depicted at oblique angles along opposing dynamic diagonal lines that cross just below the center of the composition where the figures appear. The dominant figure in this mountaintop setting is that of the "wandering miner," a tall, slender figure virtually identical in stance and dress to *The Prospector* except for a red, instead of a blue, shirt and some variants in the arrangement of his backpack. It is the second figure, seated cross-legged on a rock at the feet of the prospector, that gives this painting its greater allegorical significance. By way of contrast to the miner, the enigmatic figure of Mountain Jack is rather dwarfish, with a disproportionately large head. He, too, is heavily bearded, and simply dressed in a white shirt, gray pants, black boots, and a tattered straw hat, but unaccompanied by other character-defining paraphernalia. Jack's principal distinguishing attribute is a hand with six fingers (the thumb is not visible). There is conjecture that Mountain Jack is the artist's depiction of Six-Fingered Jack, a legendary folk character from Gold Rush mythology who was able to point to places where gold would be found. Jack's somewhat elflike image suggests a kinship to the mythical leprechaun of Irish folklore, as one who, when apprehended, can reveal hidden treasure. In Martin's allegory on the revelation of fortune, the painter imparts a knowing glint to Jack's eyes as he looks over his shoulder at the miner while pointing to some hidden site in the valley below. The theme of this painting is both iconic in its representation of the California prospector and emblematic of the perceived promise of the Gold Rush.

The now-lost third painting of the trio is known only by a brief description taken from a Sacramento newspaper published in December 1850:

> An Original Painting—E. H. Martin, Esq., the artist, has executed a most beautiful and correct portrait of the wild mountaineer of California, familiarly known as "Mountain Jack." The design represents him as loading his rifle, with his dog, panting on one side, and a dying antelope on the other. It would compensate any person to visit his office on Second Street, between J and K, to examine this together with other representations which he has happily conceived and artistically executed. Mr. Martin stands high in his profession, and the people of California should foster and encourage merit where it exists.[16]

It may be assumed that *Mountain Jack* was one of the "two large scenes upon elliptic canvases, representing *Mountain Jack and a Wandering Miner,*" mentioned in a newspaper article printed after Martin had died and attributed to his friend Dr. John Frederic Morse, the editor and founder of the *Sacramento Union,* as having been seen in Martin's studio. Martin was reportedly offered three hundred dollars for each of the scenes as he was painting them, but both works were still among his possessions at the time of his early death from cholera in 1851.

Scenes of Mining Life

Janice T. Driesbach

PROFESSIONAL ARTISTS CREATED a significant number of important paintings or drawings of Gold Rush subjects, but many other individuals also contributed to the artistic legacy of this period. Some were trained as artists, but stayed in California only briefly. Others pursued related careers as engravers or illustrators, publishing handbooks, prints, or letter sheets of mining tales and activities. Yet others probably indulged in sketching or making watercolors as a pastime to relieve the boredom and loneliness they experienced far from home. The images they recorded along riverbeds and in mining camps and towns throughout much of Northern California tend to be relatively small and on paper, but offer telling observations of mining technologies as well as Gold Rush lifestyles. For the most part, they date to the months immediately following the discovery of gold, and are valuable in reflecting the impressions of Argonauts upon their arrival in California, as well as early efforts to grapple with the challenges of finding shelter and food while attempting to procure gold under unpredictable circumstances. Most likely made for personal enjoyment, to send home, or to share with camp acquaintances, as well as for publication and mass distribution, their studies are also often impressive visually.

Among the first arrivals in California following the discovery of gold were would-be miners who were in the Caribbean or the South Pacific when word of the gold discovery spread. Nearer to California, they heard the news considerably earlier than did their colleagues on the East Coast or in Europe.

John Prendergast, an Englishman, was in Honolulu when he heard the rumors of gold. He arrived in San Francisco in July 1848, and by the following spring—when most other American and European artists were just starting out for California—was selling views of San Francisco for twenty-five dollars apiece.[1] A skilled draftsman who worked in pencil, crayon, and watercolor, Prendergast also made a number of drawings to be translated into lithographs. Among his few surviving paintings is the watercolor *San Francisco after Fire* (fig. 10), which shows the aftermath of a blaze that swept through Portsmouth Square on 22 June 1851. With the sky now clearing, the scene offers striking contrasts between the rubble of the demolished buildings and those unscathed by flames. The watercolor deftly portrays the activity: Some residents gather across from the scorched area, others make preparations for rebuilding. Tables, chairs, and other personal effects offer a focal point in the foreground, with hundreds of figures summarily indicated beyond. Prendergast ably demonstrates his ability to organize a complex subject effectively; in addition, the subtle variations in the washes used to describe buildings, shadows, and emerging daylight are to the artist's credit.

FIG. 10. John Prendergast, *San Francisco after Fire,* 1851. Watercolor on paper, 7¾ × 13¾ in. Oakland Museum of California, gift of the estate of Marjorie Eaton by exchange.

Likewise, Augusto Ferran and José Baturone disembarked in San Francisco in early 1849 from Cuba. Their best-known images of the Gold Rush are from the *Album Californiano,* popularly known as *Tipos Californianos.* This series of lithographs offers striking depictions of miners upon their return to San Francisco from forays to the goldfields (fig. 11). The images are distinctive for the vivid personalities of their subjects, which are portrayed acutely and with humor.

The twelve lithographs comprising *Album Californiano* were published as a set in Havana, an indication of the breadth of interest in the Gold Rush. Although believed to have been printed as early as 1849, the series was more likely to have been issued in 1850, after the artists could observe miners returning from the diggings in greater numbers. This is also the date on two accomplished paintings Ferran created of San Francisco (figs. 12 and 13). In both views—one a bustling city scene—the port is bathed in a glowing yellow light that unifies the compositions and endows them with a spiritual quality. In their use of light as an emotional element and in the sensitive depiction of the myriad details of the busy harbor, the paintings show parallels to the work of J. M. W. Turner and to contemporary German romantic painting.

FIG. 11. Augusto Ferran, artist, L. Marquier, publisher, *Album Californiano, 12. Realizacion. Selling Off.,* 1850. Lithograph, 10⅛ × 8 in. California Historical Society, San Francisco.

Only in late spring 1849, however, did a significant number of artists reach San Francisco. For some arrivals, gold mining seems to have been a secondary objective. Among these appears to be William McIlvaine, who received a graduate diploma in Philadelphia and studied painting in Europe. McIlvaine traveled to the Tuolumne and Merced rivers upon his arrival in California to collect material for an illustrated book on the goldfields. Published in 1850, his *Sketches of Scenery and Notes of Personal Adventure in California and Mexico,* which consists of sixteen plates as well as text, was one of the first travel accounts on the Gold Rush. *Panning Gold, California* (fig. 14) was one of the elegant watercolors that McIlvaine produced during his six-month stay in California, and may have been intended as a model for an oil painting as well as a study for an illustration.[2] In showing gold panning, McIlvaine depicts an activity widespread during the early months of the Gold Rush, when gold was more readily available, especially in the richest regions, such as along the Tuolumne River.

In McIlvaine's beautifully rendered watercolor, the mining activities fail to distract from the surrounding landscape. In contrast to the bustle of activity associated with some mining sites—as in *Miners in the Sierra* (fig. 43), for instance—the figures in *Panning Gold, California* seem quite isolated. Despite the presence of tents across the river and cattle in the distance at the left, a sense of calm pervades the composition. While one man balances his shovel on a rock and his companion studies the contents of

FIG. 12. Augusto Ferran, *San Francisco: View from the Hills to Northwest,* 1850. Oil on paper, 11⅞ × 23⅞ in. The Bancroft Library, University of California, Berkeley.

FIG. 13. Augusto Ferran, *Vista de San Francisco,* 1850. Oil on paper, 11⅞ × 23⅞ in. The Bancroft Library, University of California, Berkeley.

FIG. 14. William McIlvaine, *Panning Gold, California,* n.d. Watercolor over pencil on paper, 18⅝ × 27½ in. M. & M. Karolik Collection, courtesy of Museum of Fine Arts, Boston. 51.2534

FIG. 15. William McIlvaine, *Prairie, California,* 1854. Watercolor on paper, 19⅝ × 27 in. Gift of Maxim Karolik, courtesy Museum of Fine Arts, Boston. 53.2448

his gold pan, the spectator's eye is drawn to the steep hillsides that enclose the river in the background. Although it would seem that the water should race through such a small opening, the river—and indeed all the other elements—in McIlvaine's composition is placid. With the exception of the figures, all seems to be still, an effect reinforced by the muted pink and gold tones that dominate the composition.

Although it depicts more figures and activities, *Prairie, California* (fig. 15), created in 1854, also appears to be a sylvan scene, in part because of the space given over to the open field and undifferentiated sky. In this setting, which has been identified as being near Sonora, the small tents (one draped with an American flag) illustrate the shelters miners hastily assembled in open fields, with carts and mules acknowledging the principal means of transportation to mining sites and to acquire supplies.[3] Although McIlvaine portrays a number of figures here, the camp seems remote and sparsely populated.

In drawings such as these, McIlvaine created some of the finest early depictions of the California Gold Rush.[4] However, because he visited rural mining sites for the most part and had returned East by November 1849, his accomplishments went largely unnoticed by San Francisco's nascent art community. Back home, McIlvaine continued to make and exhibit paintings and watercolors inspired by his travels. He seems, however, to have had little influence in stimulating interest in California subjects among other eastern artists.

A number of views dating to 1849, such as W. Taber's *Steam Gold Dredger Ascending the Sacramento* (fig. 16), record historic moments, here the voyage of the first gold dredger in California. This charming drawing, which appears to have been sketched on the spot, served as the basis for an illustration that was published in *Century Magazine* over forty years later, to accompany a retrospective article on the Gold Rush.[5] The subject of Taber's vignette was a small steamboat that was shipped to San Francisco in parts by one of the first joint mining companies to leave the East Coast. Capitalizing on the large quantity of freight that could be transported by ship, Argonauts aboard the *Edward Everett* brought along parts to assemble a large scow in California. In hopes of successfully dredging along the Sacramento River and its tributaries, they constructed the stern-wheel driven vessel with a workshop to house the crew and allow space to divide the proceeds. The idea, however, proved impractical, and "so completely convinced [were] her owners of the absurdity of the scheme that they quietly dismantled and disposed of her."[6] Taber's record of this short-lived experiment shows a number of passengers in conversation on their journey upriver. Their striking silhouettes and the vivid white highlights add charm to the drawing, and contrast with the dense smoke that spews forth from the steam engine.

William Birch McMurtrie's watercolor *View of Telegraph Hill and City, North on Montgomery Street* (fig. 17), painted in late 1849, records the growth San Francisco was experiencing. The hill topped by a freshly made grave that confronts the viewer in the foreground testifies to the loss of life during the Gold Rush, but the scene is otherwise lively. Emphasis is now given to the buildings, many of which have two stories and are constructed of wood. Although somewhat crudely drawn, the scene nonetheless offers substantial information and served as a model for George Burgess's retrospective canvas *San Francisco in July, 1849* (see fig. 60).

Other artists who created early views of San Francisco include Harrison Eastman, who apparently spent only a brief period at the mines following his arrival in the fall of 1849. After the mining company with which he took passage to San Francisco disbanded, Eastman was employed at the San Francisco post office.[7] Eastman soon found time to record local urban landmarks. In his watercolor *Saint Francis Hotel, Cor. Clay and Dupont Sts.* (fig. 18), the crude lawn fronting the building documents the primitive

FIG. 16. W. Taber, *Steam Gold Dredger Ascending the Sacramento,* 1849. Ink and gouache on paper mounted on board, $4\frac{1}{4} \times 10\frac{7}{8}$ in. California Historical Society, San Francisco, gift of Lawton R. Kennedy.

FIG. 17. William Birch McMurtrie, *View of Telegraph Hill and City, North on Montgomery Street,* 1849. Watercolor and graphite on paper, 10 × 14 in. California Historical Society, San Francisco, gift of Theodora N. McMurtrie.

conditions in the city. Only recently constructed, the Saint Francis was, according to accounts, one of the few reputable hotels in the city. Judged to be "the only hotel at present where respectable ladies are taken in," the rooms were, nonetheless, separated only by cloth partitions, and therefore afforded boarders little privacy.[8] In contrast to the well-dressed party in the center of Eastman's watercolor, the adjacent tents, one bearing a "RESTAURANT" sign, give evidence of how hastily the community had been established.

Fig. 18. Harrison Eastman, *Saint Francis Hotel, Cor. Clay and Dupont Sts.,* 1849. Watercolor on paper mounted on cardboard, 9¾ × 9½ in. California Historical Society, San Francisco, gift of Templeton Crocker.

Soon after he painted *Saint Francis Hotel,* Eastman established himself as a designer and engraver. He contributed illustrations to local journals, and made a number of engravings from drawings by his close friend Charles Christian Nahl. Like other artists in California at the time, Eastman realized his greatest financial success producing prints and illustrations, first in the employ of lithographers in San Francisco and later as the co-owner of an engraving company.[9]

In addition to a demand for prints of San Francisco and mining sites, there was also some market for portraiture.

> Every man wanted a sketch of his claim, or his cabin, or some spot with which he identified himself; and as they all offered to pay very handsomely, I was satisfied that I could make paper and pencil much more profitable tools to work with than pick and shovel.[10]

Among the first portrait painters to come to notice in San Francisco was Samuel Stillman Osgood, who had studied painting in Boston and traveled to Europe before opening a successful studio in the East. Arriving in California in August 1849 to try his luck at mining, Osgood soon reverted to the career for which he was trained. He took up residence in San Francisco, where he painted a portrait of General John A. Sutter (fig. 19) from a sketch made at Sutter's Fort on his return from the goldfields. Osgood made five versions of this portrait, and took at least one of them to New York with him in November

FIG. 19. Samuel Stillman Osgood, *General John A. Sutter,* ca. 1849. Oil on bed ticking, $29\frac{1}{8} \times 23\frac{3}{4}$ in. Fine Arts Museums of San Francisco, Museum Purchase. 54768

1849. John Sartain used it to create an engraving of Sutter. The print was popular in the East, bringing Osgood considerable attention.

Osgood shows his subject wearing a white shirt, jacket, and tied scarf, rather than the military attire Sutter chose for later portraits. Seated gazing toward his left, Sutter is sympathetically portrayed. He is formally posed, but with an alert countenance. The monochromatic background focuses all attention on the subject, who appears both lifelike and approachable. This portrait appears modest in comparison to William Smith Jewett's later depictions of this pioneer (see figs. 37 and 38).

A quite different portrait subject is depicted in *A Lucky Striker,* by an artist known only by the initials "A. G." (fig. 20). Although the head of the fortunate miner is outsized in proportion to his body, the expressive face and the sensitively rendered landscape background suggest he was painted by a skilled hand. The pose and details of the features suggest that the painter may have worked from a daguerreotype model. Nonetheless, the figure is presented with immediacy. As was common in photographs, the miner is dressed in a workshirt and holds a pick. His neatly combed hair and beard and fresh garments have more in common with the appearance of prospective miners than with descriptions of those working claims. And the large gold nugget the young man holds may reflect his aspirations rather than any success in the placer country. However, as the welded gold pan at the left indicates, this view was recorded early in the Gold Rush period, and the subject may indeed be one of the favored early arrivals whose labors were amply rewarded.

FIG. 20. Artist unknown, "A. G." *A Lucky Striker,* n.d. Watercolor on cardboard, 6¾ × 5¾ in. Collection of Dr. Oscar and Trudy Lemer.

Another early image is John Henry Dunnel's *Sutter's Mill at Coloma* (fig. 22), made a number of months after he first arrived in the mining regions. Dated 1850, this watercolor offers a visual record of

FIG. 21. Washington F. Friend, *Placer Mining,* n.d. Watercolor on paper, 12⅛ × 16⅛ in. The Bancroft Library, University of California, Berkeley.

FIG. 22. John Henry Dunnel, *Sutter's Mill at Coloma,* 1850. Watercolor on illustration board, 8⅝ × 6¾ in. The Bancroft Library, University of California, Berkeley.

how thoroughly the land around the site where James Marshall discovered gold was excavated in the initial mining season. In this scene, the tailrace in which gold was first spotted has been diverted, but the mill is not yet enclosed. The lumber stacked in the background attests to the other commercial activity that took place at this spot.

Washington F. Friend's watercolor *Placer Mining* (fig. 21) is undated, but likely made no earlier than 1850, as the mining activity is focused around a variety of sluice box or long tom. This device, which had an iron sieve at one end, allowed miners to wash dirt continuously without having to remove their equipment from the water. Although offering much greater speed, the long tom also required miners to work together in groups. Mining thus rapidly became a joint venture, no longer the individual effort that William McIlvaine had recorded in 1849 in *Panning Gold, California* (see fig. 14). Friend's watercolor, perhaps made in preparation for the panorama he was undertaking, represents a prospecting operation at a likely location along a ledge where a rock outcropping juts into the river.[11]

The challenge of mining for gold after the easily accessible flakes and nuggets had been removed in the early months of the Gold Rush is reflected in images showing increasingly complex technologies requiring group efforts. *Mining Scene: Diverting a River* (fig. 23) by an unidentified artist, shows an ambitious operation, in which many miners are working together to uncover an old riverbed that lies beneath a substantial layer of overburden. Here they gather to "bench out" the overlying ground with picks and shovels. The beauty of the watercolor, in which houses and large oaks underneath a clear sky in the distance form a secondary center of interest, contrasts with the arduous labor shown in the foreground. That earth is being removed by hand, rather than washed away by the force of water, indicates that this scene was encountered before 1852, when much more efficient hydraulic mining methods would have been used.[12]

Mining in California (fig. 24), also by an unidentified artist, shows the process of mining quicksilver, which began in California even before gold was discovered, and became increasingly important as the Gold Rush progressed. At New Almaden, fifteen miles southeast of San Jose, quicksilver occurred in scattered deposits, and was being extracted by 1846. The first quicksilver concentration discovered in North America, the New Almaden mines were distinguished by the abundance and high mercury content of their ore. Miners used quicksilver when extracting gold in combination with other elements as it amalgamates with gold but evaporates when heated, allowing gold to be collected easily. The availability of quicksilver nearby at New Almaden is credited with greatly enhancing the quantity of gold taken from the Sierra and reducing the cost of its recovery. Unlike gold mining, however, the process of isolating quicksilver from the cinnabar in which it occurs naturally required considerable technology, which was introduced into California by the Mexican workforce at New Almaden.[13] *Mining in California* shows the furnaces used to heat cinnabar at the left middle ground; above and to the right lies the mill where the product was pulverized. The drawing most likely dates to around 1853 when "six furnaces with a capacity of 15,000 pounds of ore were kept going day and night. Seven or eight days were required for one furnace operation—charging, firing, and discharging."[14] The beauty of *Mining in California,* with its delicate washes and careful notations of the Mexican workers and their families along the pathways and in communal areas, belies the perils of processing quicksilver. Little would the viewer of this lovely scene suspect that "the men working at the furnaces were so much

FIG. 23. Artist unknown, *Mining Scene: Diverting a River,* n.d. Watercolor on paper, 12×9 in. Collection of Dr. Oscar and Trudy Lemer.

FIG. 24. Artist unknown, *Mining in California,* n.d. Watercolor on paper, 12½ × 18 in. The Gilcrease Museum, Tulsa, Okla.

affected by the noxious vapors that they were kept at work three or four weeks only, after which a fresh set of workmen were put in their place."[15]

Among those who joined the Gold Rush for reasons other than to acquire mineral wealth was John Woodhouse Audubon. Admitting that his interest was piqued by the remarkable tales of gold he heard, Audubon also recalled his father's admonition while he had been in Texas in 1845 to "Push on to California, [where] you will find new animals and birds at every change in the formation of the country, and birds from Central America will delight you." He joined Colonel Webb's California Company, and because of his "backwoods experience" was selected as second-in-command of the ill-fated group, which—in wanting to get an early start—chose a less popular route via New Orleans and northern Mexico to the Pacific.[16] Leaving in February 1849, the party, inexperienced in wilderness travel, was ravaged by cholera and robbed of nearly half its assets in Mexico. Audubon was unable to pursue his scientific or artistic interests during his journey.[17] It was only when they stopped so each man might celebrate the Fourth of July holiday as he pleased that Audubon "unpacked . . . paper and pencils" and made his first surviving sketch from his journey through Mexico.[18] Two weeks later in a remote region some 160 miles northeast of Guadalajara, his *Twenty-Five Miles West of Jesus Maria* (fig. 25) shows his group's encampment in a broad valley beneath looming sandstone outcroppings. The fine detail given to the tents, figures, and trees amongst the broad watercolor washes attests to Audubon's considerable skills as a draftsman.

Arriving in California nine months after their journey began, Audubon's company encountered rain-soaked mining camps and astronomical prices. Assessing their situation (they were "in a forlorn condition, almost without clothes"), Audubon felt responsible for helping recoup the group's losses. He explained that ". . . though I never intended to go to the mines myself, I feel now for the sake of the men who stood by me, that I must stay by them." This comment is followed by the complaint that "my paints

FIG. 25. John Woodhouse Audubon, *Twenty-five Miles West of Jesus Maria,* 1850. Watercolor and pencil on paper, 10¼ × 13 in. Southwest Museum, Los Angeles, gift of Eva Scott Fenyes. 22.G.978AB

and canvas have been left on the desert, my few specimens lost or thrown away; and lack of time, and the weakness produced by my two illnesses . . . , and the monotonous food, have robbed me of all enthusiasm."[19]

Thus Audubon set out with a number of his party for the southern mines early in the new year. In the ensuing weeks, Audubon visited a number of camps, where he made drawings and written observations about the surrounding landscape and mining life. His depiction of a leafless oak in *Murphy's New Diggings* (fig. 26), made on 9 February 1850, demonstrates Audubon's fondness for trees and the attention he gave his drawings, even when they were made under adverse circumstances. Although beautifully rendered, the scene is bleak. Audubon voiced his discouragement in his journal entry the following day: "Everything seems against us—weather and season, water and rain, interrupt us in all our attempts at work, and ill-luck seems to follow us."[20] *Murphy's New Diggings* is characteristic of Audubon's pencil drawings in offering considerable detail, and in the color notations and comments inscribed on it. These indicate that Audubon intended to use them as studies for watercolors or paintings. Although he occasionally included figures, for the most part—as here—Audubon described trees or significant land forms. In effect, his acutely recorded drawings are illustrations, giving little evidence of the turmoil that accompanied his trip or the effects on the travelers of the spectacular landscape vistas he described in his journal.

FIG. 26. John Woodhouse Audubon, *Murphy's New Diggings (Oak of the Hills),* ca. 1850. Pencil on paper, 10¼ × 13 in. Southwest Museum, Los Angeles, gift of Eva Scott Fenyes. 22.G.978D

The beauty of his drawing *Hawkin's Bar* (fig. 27) also belies the frustration Audubon must have felt in late spring, when the previous winter's snow left the mining site still submerged. Nevertheless, his interests as an artist prevailed, and soon abundant foliage attracted his attention; "leaving Hawkin's Bar for Green Springs, we sauntered along the trail under the beautiful post-oaks, just now in their greatest beauty, with leaves half-grown and pendant catkins."[21]

Although Audubon was frustrated in his efforts to make oil paintings of the surrounding landscapes, his tour of the mining regions was rewarded by his success in making "nearly ninety careful sketches, and many hasty ones."[22] Similarly, he kept his sketchbook close at hand when returning from his trek, recording his brief stays in Sacramento and San Francisco in several sensitive drawings. *Sacramento City* (fig. 28) appears to be more a small village than a thriving supply center, with animals

FIG. 27. John Woodhouse Audubon, *Hawkin's Bar,* 1850. Pencil on paper, 10¼ × 13 in. Southwest Museum, Los Angeles, gift of Eva Scott Fenyes. 22.G.9786

FIG. 28. John Woodhouse Audubon, *Sacramento City,* 1850. Pencil on paper, 10¼ × 13 in. Southwest Museum, Los Angeles, gift of Eva Scott Fenyes. 22.G.978AA

FIG. 29. John Woodhouse Audubon, *San Francisco,* 1850. Pencil on paper, 10¼ × 13 in. Southwest Museum, Los Angeles, gift of Eva Scott Fenyes. 22.G.978V

grazing in the foreground, an unhitched covered wagon resting at the left center, and only a few buildings in sight. A stack of boards partially obscures the lightly sketched masts of a boat, the only reference to the harbor. Although several figures stand about, they are relatively small and unobtrusive. The large trees, which are rendered in considerable detail, appear of greater interest to Audubon.

In contrast, *San Francisco* (fig. 29), a view from Nob Hill showing Yerba Buena Cove and anchorage, drawn little more than a month later (30 May 1850), shows an array of buildings—both residences and commercial establishments—crowded against the waterfront. Although still endowed with a sense of calm, instilled by the motionless water and barren hills in the background, the numerous structures clustered around Long Wharf (which projects into the bay at the center) give compelling evidence of urban development.

Another pioneer artist best known as an illustrator is Francis Samuel Marryat, an Englishman who used part of his father's bequest to finance his trip to California in 1850. Marryat had previously published an account of his travels in *Borneo and the Indian Archipelago,* and recorded this journey in his *Mountains and Molehills,* published in 1855. He kept a diary and made drawings for this purpose, many of which perished in the San Francisco fire of 22 June 1851, recorded by John Prendergast (see fig. 10). Marryat also witnessed several of the fires that broke out in San Francisco with some regularity, and just a few months after he arrived in California recorded one in a watercolor, *San Francisco Fire of 17 September 1850* (fig. 30). At least the second such conflagration the artist witnessed; Marryat's view shows the large buildings, many four stories tall, that now occupied San Francisco's business district, and the readiness of the volunteer fire companies that had formed in response to the number of fires that had broken out. His watercolor is enlivened not only by the billowing clouds of smoke that rise from the distant buildings, but also by the depictions of onlookers and scattered piles of their belongings in the foreground.

Undaunted, the settlers rebuilt the city after each fire, and E. Godchaux's gouache *Vue de San-Francisco en 1851* (fig. 31), recorded the following year, demonstrates their success. Indeed, in this view, San Francisco boasts four long wharves and a fair number of wooden structures. Here there are no indications of the campsites evident in earlier depictions, and human activity is limited. With his tender rendering of the trees and grasses in the foreground, it seems likely that this otherwise unknown artist was more interested in depicting the landscape. Scenes such as Audubon, Marryat, and Godchaux described are thus important in documenting the evolution of the early Gold Rush, and deepen our understanding of the experiences encountered by the artists and of events in California at the time.

FIG. 30. Francis Samuel Marryat, *San Francisco Fire of 17 September 1850,* 1850. Watercolor on paper, 9⅜ × 13½ in. Oakland Museum of California, Kahn Collection.

FIG. 31. E. Godchaux, *Vue de San-Francisco en 1851,* 1851. Gouache on paper, 10 × 16 in. Garzoli Gallery, San Rafael, Calif.

FIG. 32. William Smith Jewett, *Captain Washington A. Bartlett, U.S.N.,* 1850. Oil on canvas, 22 × 18 in. California Historical Society, San Francisco.

Portrait Painter to the Elite

WILLIAM SMITH JEWETT

Janice T. Driesbach

LATE IN 1849 SAN FRANCISCO gained its first resident professional painter when William Smith Jewett arrived on 17 December. Like many Argonauts, Jewett had traveled with a mining company, which broke up shortly after their ship reached port. The adventurers' arrival amidst heavy rains, which soaked the city to the extent that "everything . . . here looks as though it had been shaken into a complete jelly," delayed their progress to the goldfields.[1]

Jewett had met with mixed success in his practice in the East,[2] but within six weeks of his arrival in California he reported securing a number of commissions. Although he had surely expected to acquire wealth mining or in a related business venture, Jewett profited as a painter before he had an opportunity even to try his luck at mining. Most likely he discovered that his talents were in greater demand and offered him more substantial remuneration than they had in his native New York, where there was more competition for patrons. In letters, Jewett reported encountering many acquaintances from home, who "have all insisted so strongly upon my sitting up my easel right amongst all this crazy stuff that I have at last done so and am at work quite in earnest."[3] Interestingly, although Jewett's correspondence makes it clear that throughout most of his long residency in San Francisco he envisioned returning home imminently, he did not exhibit his work in the East while he was in California.[4] By January 1850, he was reporting enthusiastically about his reception:

> Society has great hopes of *me* here and think I am a lucky fall to them, gentlemen desire their portraits to send home to their families and I am likely to be full of work I paint very rapid take them on the wing and all are profesighing [*sic*] a fracture to my hand.[5]

Not only was the artist quickly fulfilling orders, but also his talents caught the attention of California's leading political figures. Jewett had requests from California's governor and lieutenant governor, among others. Expecting that he could complete two or three portraits each week, for between $150 and $800 each, he declared himself "as jolly . . . as a clam at high water."[6] Financial transactions were conducted in hard currency. With the silver he received in return for a portrait, Jewett had to face the problem for "the first time in my life" of what to do with his money. "So I came home and got a large canvas bag I had used for common trapsticks went back and I shoveled it into it and lugged it home." Likewise, he noted, costs were astronomical. Nonetheless, Jewett speculated that if business were pursued energetically, "a fortune can be made speedily."[7] He had already profited on a sale of real estate, the first of many such investments Jewett undertook during his twenty-year stay in California, and his detailed reports in letters home suggest that his business ventures were as important to him as the progress of his painting was.

On 30 January 1850 Jewett announced he "made fifty dollars today in painting one little head at one sitting" and noted that "there are other artists here and doing comparably nothing some do not endeavor to paint at all, I somehow appear to be popular and don't know why. "[8] Among the projects he was offered was a panorama of California; despite the promise of a considerable sum of money, Jewett viewed the undertaking as "a most uncongenial task for my mind."[9] This response is somewhat surprising, given his professed interest in visiting the mining regions in coming months to make sketches. However, the vast scale of a panorama may have struck the artist as onerous; also—ever-conscious of his economic prospects—he noted that another artist was already engaged on a similar undertaking. In any case, his work was in sufficient demand that he could turn away commissions that did not appeal to him.[10]

Within two months, his talents were noted in the local press, with the *Alta California* declaring enthusiastically:

> We have had quite a number of amateur painters visit our good city, some of whom could make a very *pretty* picture, without much regard to accuracy or a striking delineation of the faces and figures of their subjects. Now, however, we have an "artist as is an artist" here, who can paint a *likeness* of a person as well as a finished picture. We allude to Mr. Jewett from New York, who has his studio on Clay Street, where we yesterday saw the portraits of several of our first citizens, and it is with pleasure that we recommend him to the public.[11]

In adding that "any one desirous to send a portrait to the States can have it put in a tin case by Mr. J. in very compact form for transmission," the *Alta* acknowledged the widespread interest in sending portraits to distant family members and friends.[12]

Among the projects Jewett undertook at this time was his portrait of the Grayson family, *The Promised Land* (fig. 33). Although it is uncertain how the artist met the Graysons, it is likely that they were introduced by mutual friends. Andrew Jackson Grayson and his wife had long intended their arrival in California four years earlier to be commemorated in a painting, and Jewett appears to have been commissioned in January 1850. The artist received both a substantial fee (two thousand dollars) and detailed instructions from the Graysons. They requested not only that Jewett visit the scene in person, but also, in an ambitious composition, include numerous themes and motifs, such as "success of pioneers; threatening mountains; smiling valley, three full-length portraits, Grayson in buckskin outfit

Mrs. Grayson made for him; her own horse, saddle, utensils; the woodsman's gun, and the forest."[13]

Despite the incentive this commission offered, Jewett delayed venturing into the Sierra foothills to make sketches until after his lodgings in San Francisco were destroyed by fire in early May 1850. He then proceeded to Coloma, where he first visited another patron, John T. Little, and tried his hand at mining. Only toward the end of the month did Jewett meet up with Grayson to make sketches at a site now identified as Hotchkiss Hill near Georgetown.[14] From there he returned first to Coloma, and later to San Francisco, where he completed the painting.

FIG. 33. William Smith Jewett, *The Promised Land—The Grayson Family,* 1850. Oil on canvas, 50¾ × 64 in. Daniel J. Terra Collection, courtesy of Terra Museum of American Art, Chicago. 5.1994

Jewett ingeniously organized the figures in *The Promised Land* in a pyramidal configuration, with Grayson standing at the center of the canvas. Mrs. Grayson and their young son, dressed in an ermine-trimmed coat that reflected the immigrants' aspirations rather than the apparel of overland travelers, are seated to the right in a pose reminiscent of depictions of the Mother and Child in the Rest on the Flight into Egypt by such artists as Claude Lorrain.[15] With the menacing snow-packed peak looming behind them, the settlers pause to ponder the sweeping landscape that welcomes them into the Sacramento Valley. The image Jewett crafted, with its myriad references, secured the artist's reputation in California. A subject of discussion even while it was being painted, *The Promised Land* was an instant success; in it "fellow pioneers in the California adventure immediately recognized a symbol of themselves."[16]

More common among Jewett's commissions were portraits of individuals. Among his early efforts is the painting *Captain Washington A. Bartlett, U.S.N.* (fig. 32), which the artist exhibited at the National Academy of Design in New York in 1851. Bartlett was San Francisco's first alcalde, or mayor, and his short tenure (from September 1846 to February 1847) was distinguished by the change of the city's name from Yerba Buena. Afterward, Bartlett returned to military duties, but remained a prominent San Francisco citizen. The portrait was most likely one of a series Jewett was making as part of a gallery of notables that he hoped to sell to the state of California. The project was abandoned after the fire in May 1851 destroyed the portraits in Jewett's studio.[17] In the detailed features of the subject and the setting with a column and a red velvet curtain in the background, the small half-length format painting is consistent with other portraits Jewett made of San Francisco's leading politicians.

Other portraits made at this time suggest that Jewett also favored landscape backgrounds to complement his subjects and as focal points in their own right. This may reflect an interest he developed while in the East, where he had exhibited landscapes, and his response to California's impressive geographic features.[18] The author of a glowing review of a portrait, *Colonel Collier* (location unknown), with the subject standing on the north side of Telegraph Hill, for example, acknowledged the landscape background in recommending the painting to the viewer.[19]

By 1851, Jewett had also completed a portrait of John A. Sutter (location unknown), a man who figured prominently in his work during the years that followed. Jewett not only recorded Sutter several times during the 1850s, but also painted two views of Hock Farm, Sutter's ranch north of Sacramento (figs. 34 and 35). These paintings were created in rapid succession (1851 and 1852), and are distinguished only by differences in minor figures and the presence of a steamboat at the distant right in the earlier version, *Hock Farm (A View of the Butte Mountains from Feather River, California)* (Oakland Museum of California). Both compositions show a dog running up to two men upon their arrival along (or departure from) the shore of the Feather River. Although a focal point, the purpose of the visitors' business is unclear; likewise, the idyllic scenes fail to show the "redwood mansion" that Sutter had reportedly built at Hock Farm in 1849, or the "vineyards, orchards, and gardens of rare plants and shrubs" he maintained there.[20] Instead, a crude wood structure beside a vegetable plot draws the eye to the left middle ground, behind which cattle graze on the higher land and the Sutter Buttes appear in the distance. In both versions, the organization of the landscape into foreground, middle ground, and background planes and the detailed rendering of the foliage demonstrate the artist's Hudson River school training. Jewett pays particular attention to the depiction of the trees along the riverbank and to the foreground figures, and again employs a compositional scheme reminiscent of the paintings of Claude. The tree stumps in the left foreground are, however, outsized in relation to other objects and Jewett seems ill at ease in rendering the distant buttes. Possibly one version of *Hock Farm* was intended to be published as a lithograph as Sarony and Major had reproduced Jewett's view of Sutter's Mill and Coloma Valley for distribution in 1851. That image had been taken from a painting Jewett had sketched at Coloma, which was praised by the San Francisco *Daily Alta California* as "exceedingly truthful and beautiful." The resulting print garnered considerable attention: "It is wonderfully minute and accurate, so creditable to

FIG. 34. William Smith Jewett, *Hock Farm (A View of the Butte Mountains from Feather River, California),* 1851. Oil on canvas, 28 × 39 in. Oakland Museum of California, gift of an anonymous donor.

FIG. 35. William Smith Jewett, *Hock Farm,* 1852. Oil on canvas, 29 × 40 in. Courtesy of California State Parks, Museum Resource Center.

FIG. 36. William Smith Jewett, *Captain Ned Wakeman,* ca. 1851. Oil on canvas, 18¾ × 16 in. Oakland Museum of California, gift of Mr. and Mrs. Howard Willoughby and Mr. and Mrs. Edgar Buttner.

the true artist from whose pencil and brush it came, a fresh counterpart of nature."[21]

For the most part, however, Jewett is known primarily for his many portraits of Gold Rush luminaries. An example of his informal portrait style is represented in his engaging portrait, *Captain Ned Wakeman* (fig. 36). Wakeman had captured public attention when he sailed the *New World* out of New York Harbor while his vessel was occupied by United States marshals, depositing the law enforcement officers at Sandy Hook, and proceeding on his voyage. For a number of years the colorful sailor, who was the model for the ship's master in several stories by Mark Twain, commanded ships sailing to mining supply centers, and served with distinction on San Francisco's vigilante force. Jewett shows Wakeman aboard a vessel during a storm at night. He draws attention to the sailor's face by the windswept hair, amount of detail, and the bright light that is focused on it. Other centers of interest in the painting are the gold filigree pin on Wakeman's shirt and the horn, or speaking trumpet, he holds. The trumpet was a gift to Wakeman from the Committee on Vigilance in 1851 in recognition of his contributions.[22] Speaking trumpets, associated with firemen and sea captains, who used them for communications, were embellished and presented as gifts during the Gold Rush. They were very popular at the time, and accounted for much of the business received by San Francisco's many resident jewelers. Although Francis Marryat protested that they had become ubiquitous, Wakeman nonetheless took obvious pride in his honor.[23]

Despite the arrival of Charles Christian Nahl, his half-brother, Arthur Nahl, and August Wenderoth—all three professionally trained painters—and the enthusiastic reception that Ayres's paintings received, in 1854 William Smith Jewett was viewed as the "leading professor among us," with credit given not only to his great merit, but also to the fact "that there are Californians of taste enough to keep him constantly employed."[24] This comment reinforces the impression Jewett gave in his letters that, although there were no galleries and few exhibitions in San Francisco, artists—at least the most highly regarded—found adequate opportunities to market their skills.

Jewett did encounter resistance while achieving one of his most notable accomplishments: a full-length portrait of Sutter (fig. 37) commissioned by the state of California in 1855. He had understood initially that he would receive five thousand dollars for the painting, an extraordinary amount at the time, but when the contract was drawn up in April 1855, Jewett was awarded only twenty-five hundred dollars. He was then also asked to provide a second painting, of General Wool, without additional recompense.[25] If the additional request were not enough, Governor John Bigler approved the contract "with great reluctance." In terms reminiscent of the debates that took place in commissioning artwork for the United States Capitol, Bigler declared not only that "the amount appropriated I regarded as exceeding the value of the labor performed," but also that "the financial condition of the State does not, in my opinion, warrant expenditures for objects which can, without detriment to public interests be dispensed with for a time."[26]

On 21 October 1855, the *Sacramento Daily Bee* printed an open letter from Jewett, indicating that he felt compelled to document the completion of the painting for the state: "I have finished your full-length portrait and I shall present it before the Legislature on Monday next 19th, for their action upon it, hoping only for a slight remuneration sufficient to [defray?] my outlay as I have had it elegantly framed."[27]

FIG. 37. William Smith Jewett, *Portrait of General John A. Sutter,* 1855. Oil on canvas, 118 × 87 in. Courtesy of California State Parks, Museum Resource Center.

Jewett's portrait shows an aging, yet dignified and confident Sutter, attired in dress uniform. The general balances a sword in his right hand, and holds an elaborately plumed helmet. His bright eyes and flushed cheeks suggest an alert and robust figure, and offer no hint of the troubles that had befallen him by the time this image was created. The immediacy of the depiction attests to the numerous times the general posed for Jewett, sittings that lasted several hours apiece.[28] The cursory landscape background, with Sutter's Fort at the right, appears to have been sketched independently. Not only does it lack detail, but also the perspective of the setting—with a large tree in the left foreground overpowering the figures of a guard and a white steed—is out of scale with Sutter himself. The composition shares the incongruities present in Jewett's scenes of Hock Farm, but lacks their bright colors and detail. In addition to documenting the challenges that landscape views could present Jewett, the schematic treatment of the setting may reflect the short time allotted Jewett to complete the large portrait and his assumption that, once installed in the state capitol, the painting would be viewed at a distance.

A bust-length *Portrait of General John A. Sutter* (fig. 38), which Jewett executed the following year, also shows Sutter in the uniform of a major-general of the California militia, a public honor that had been bestowed upon him by the legislature in February 1853.[29] Again, his garments belie Sutter's precarious economic circumstances. Although Jewett's presentation of the general is a striking likeness of the man, the shallow background with the classical devices of a drawn red curtain and a column repeats the conventional treatment used in the portrait of Bartlett.

By late 1856, Jewett was perceived, according to an article that appeared in the *Daily Alta California,* as "eminently successful" in San Francisco, and his patrons were credited with possessing "a refined and cultivated taste." Although his portraits were mentioned first in the commentary, the author bestowed his highest praise on a recently completed canvas, *The Light of the Cross* (location unknown). The religious theme and interior setting of the subject were departures for Jewett, and its favorable reception was induced at least in part by its potential to educate viewers.[30]

Jewett's foray into this new subject matter may have been inspired by a commission he was given or by an interest in expanding his repertoire. *The Light of the Cross* was well received; however, the artist does not appear to have undertaken other religious themes during his stay in California. The theme of *J. E. Murdoch as Hamlet* (location unknown), from this time as well, was also a departure for the artist. Other surviving paintings from the 1860s are predominantly portraits, whose subjects included Don Juan Temple and his wife, Rafaela Cota de Temple (in the collection of La Casa de Rancho Los Cerritos, Long Beach, California), and Commodore James Thomas Watkins (Chrysler Museum, Norfolk, Virginia).

When the *First Industrial Exhibition of the Mechanics' Institute* opened in San Francisco in September 1857, William Smith Jewett was well represented in the art section, in keeping with his reputation. His contributions included eight oil portraits, *The Light of the Cross,* and *J. E. Murdoch as Hamlet.* In addition, his *Promised Land* of 1850 (cat. 33), already well known, was at last placed on public display in California.

By the late 1850s, Jewett, like a number of other artists, had ventured to Yosemite to depict the spectacular scenery. His *Yosemite Falls* (fig. 39) is an accomplished landscape and offers charming detail,

FIG. 38. William Smith Jewett, *Portrait of General John A. Sutter,* 1856. Oil on canvas, 15½ × 12½ in. Oakland Museum of California, Kahn Collection.

FIG. 39. William Smith Jewett, *Yosemite Falls,* 1859. Oil on canvas, 52½ × 42 in. Newark Museum, N.J., gift of Mrs. Charles W. Engelhard.

despite its somewhat stiff composition. Jewett also explored other new subjects at this time, including a large canvas titled *Pursued* (fig. 40), which the artist donated to the Ladies Christian Commission Fair auction in 1864.

Although Jewett continued to conduct an active portrait practice in California into the 1860s, much of his energy was devoted to real estate and other financial transactions. Now headquartered in San Francisco, he also traveled to Sacramento to fulfill commissions, spending at least three weeks there on one occasion. Jewett described that trip enthusiastically ("they give me a cheerful welcome and pay well"), but repeatedly expressed his longing to see his friends and family in the East. Nonetheless, he delayed his departure time and again, because of his financial ventures and the commissions he continued to undertake. The artist still boasted of his popularity, and tried to reassure relatives of his continuing affection for them.[31] For reasons that are not entirely clear—perhaps concern that he had not met his family's (or his own) expectations, or reluctance to return home having been so long away—Jewett did not leave San Francisco until fall 1869. The artist thus spent most of his career in California, where his well-received portraits document both the appearance and success of his early pioneer patrons. These animated paintings attest not only to the affluence of his sitters, but also to their confidence and physical well-being. In thus fulfilling the expectations of his clients, Jewett's portraits offer insights into their values as well as their features. In addition, as a skilled artist who had earned his credentials in the East, Jewett reassured early San Franciscans of the taste they displayed and acknowledged their support for culture.

FIG. 40. William Smith Jewett, *Pursued,* 1863. Oil on canvas, 29 × 36 in. Autry Museum of Western Heritage, Los Angeles.

The Hessian Party

CHARLES CHRISTIAN NAHL, ARTHUR NAHL, AND AUGUST WENDEROTH

Harvey L. Jones

Portraiture, genre painting, illustration, lithography, graphic design, and photography were among the various art services that the Nahls, Charles Christian, and his half-brother, Hugo Wilhelm Arthur, known as Arthur, and a family friend, Frederick August Wenderoth, offered to a Gold Rush clientele. Until they arrived in 1851, no artist in California possessed the high quality of European academic art training or the depth of professional and technical experience that these three men brought to an extensive range of artistic enterprises. The Nahls, from the city of Kassel, in Hesse, in what is now west central Germany, were descendants of a prominent German family of artists that extended in a continuous line back to the seventeenth century.

Leaving Kassel because of political turmoil, this Hessian party went first to Paris and then, because of unrest in France, to New York. Hearing of gold, they continued west to California. There, they purchased, naively, a salted claim in the vicinity of Rough and Ready, a notorious mining camp. Reverting to their metier, Charles briefly went into partnership with a sign painter and Arthur took a job with a woodcarver nearby. Before the end of the year Charles had established his family's home in Sacramento and opened a studio with August Wenderoth. The activities of their first studio were discussed in an article in the *Illustrated Placer Times and Transcript,* dated 1 January 1852.

> The number of orders they have recently received for paintings of various kinds has induced them to forgo their determination of removing to the Bay. An opportunity is now offered the citizens of Sacramento to gratify their taste for this exalted branch of the fine arts, in procuring pictures of such character as will constitute most pleasing momentos [*sic*] of early times in California. For admirable design and most finished execution, Mr. Nahl and Mr. Wenderoth are equally distinguished, and their works embracing a large scope of California incidents and scenery, are justly entitled to rank with the very best production of the day. In the department of portrait painting, these artists have attained a no less degree of excellence. Their likenesses are strikingly correct and possess that important recommendation as to price, which places a domestic luxury within the reach of the most moderate means. The miniatures taken by Messrs. Nahl and Wenderoth have been several times noticed and are universally admired and commended.[1]

FIG. 41. Frederick August Wenderoth, *Portrait of a Man* (unidentified), 1854. Miniature, watercolor on ivory, 4 × 3 in. Oakland Museum of California, gift of the estate of Edna B. Lake.

It has been speculated that the miniatures referred to in the article may actually have been photographs, but there is no evidence that Nahl or Wenderoth were themselves photographers. Frederick August Wenderoth's small *Portrait of a Man* (fig. 41), for example, is an exquisitely detailed, delicate watercolor, painted on wafer-thin ivory, that was probably drawn from a daguerreotype image. Its presentation in a cased oval format further enhances its association with early photographic portraiture.

Few examples of collaborative works produced by Nahl and Wenderoth survive, but among them are two lithographs, both from 1852 and signed: "Painted and Drawn on Stone by Ch Nahl & A Wenderoth." One is titled *Miner's Cabin, Result of the Day* (Oakland Museum of California) and the other *A Miner Prospecting*. The subjects of both lithographs are significant for their portrayal of the lives of gold miners in vivid images that inform two later works, *Saturday Night in the Mines,* 1856 (fig. 42)[2] by Charles Christian Nahl in collaboration with Arthur Nahl, and *The Lone Prospector,* 1853 (see fig. 61), by A. D. O. Browere.

Saturday Night in the Mines, and a companion work also painted in 1856, *Crossing the Plains* (Stanford University Museum of Art), that measures approximately ten by sixteen feet, are the two largest of the Nahl canvases extant. *Crossing the Plains* depicts an immigrant party during a pause on their exhausting journey in an ox-drawn covered wagon. The two scenes were painted in oil on yards of seamed canvas using broad brushstrokes and techniques and equipment modified to accommodate special problems in drawing and proportion that occur when working on such a large scale. A large shed was built behind Nahl's house in San Francisco for work on paintings of this size. Huge paintings of this type were popular at the time as mural decorations for hotels, saloons, and public halls. These two paintings were first displayed in a saloon in Sacramento, and then exhibited at the California State Fair in Marysville in 1858,

FIG. 42. Charles Christian Nahl and Hugo Wilhelm Arthur Nahl, *Saturday Night at the Mines,* 1856. Oil on canvas, 136 × 208 in. Stanford University Museum of Art, Stanford, Calif., gift of Jane Lathrop Stanford. 12083

before going on extended view at the state capitol.[3] Both the lithograph, *Miner's Cabin,* and the painting, *Saturday Night in the Mines,* depict the nighttime interior of a small cabin, probably much like the Nahls' cabin at Rough and Ready. Illuminated by firelight, the six miners, some of whom seem to be typical members of a recurring cast of characters in lithographs and paintings by Nahl, are engaged in various activities.

The largest of the three surviving examples with the joint signatures of Charles Nahl and August Wenderoth is the painting *Miners in the Sierra* (fig. 43), which was probably painted in their studio in Sacramento between the fall of 1851 and the fire of 2 November 1852 that destroyed much of the city. Another painting of the same size, pendant to that work but now lost, depicted Native Americans. Both paintings had been in the collection of the Fred Heilbron family, which has been prominent in Sacramento since the Gold Rush. *Miners in the Sierra* may be the first important painting of a mining scene based on the artists' own experiences at Rough and Ready, although the figures in the picture are not known to represent any particular members of the Nahl party. This work has the further distinction of being the only large-scale painting associated with Nahl that is predominantly a landscape.

FIG. 43. Charles Christian Nahl and Frederick August Wenderoth, *Miners in the Sierra,* 1851. Oil on canvas, 54¼ × 67 in. National Museum of American Art, Smithsonian Institution, Washington, D.C., gift of the Fred Heilbron Collection.

It is not known how the artists divided the labors in their collaborative efforts. It would be tempting to assume that Wenderoth was responsible for the landscape because Nahl, in his genre paintings, usually relegates landscape to secondary importance. However, as both Nahl and Wenderoth shared a common German academic training that emphasized figural compositions and because there are no known landscapes by Wenderoth, there is little evidence to support that argument.

Although the artists have presented what at first appears to be a landscape with figures, it is actually a genre subject. *Miners in the Sierra* presents an imposing mountain landscape that is as important as the depiction of the miners in a scene that may best be viewed as a Gold Rush narrative. The central placement of the mountain stream has both compositional and thematic significance. All the pictorial components are arranged along diagonal lines that converge in the center of the painting where the stream first appears above the cascade. This establishes the crucial subjective importance of the water flow in the process of sluicing for gold—as well as a stabilizing anchor for the dynamic composition. The rocky topography of the rugged landscape is somewhat softened by verdant vegetation accentuated by a few wildflowers. The distant cabin contributes a domesticating effect to the scene. With the comforting warmth of chimney smoke, the miners' wash drying on a clothesline and over nearby bushes, and the pathway of steps descending to the stream, the artists have imparted a note of optimism to the impression of harsh reality derived from their own prospecting experiences.

This picture points up the fact that by the time these artists arrived in California, gold mining typically was no longer a matter of the lone prospector panning by a stream; out of necessity finding gold became a somewhat mechanized group effort. The principal activity depicted in the painting involves four miners hard at work along either side of the long tom (a structural apparatus used to wash the gold from rocks and sand). The observer's eye is immediately drawn to the red-, white-, and blue-shirted miners whose vigorous labors with pick and shovel are well executed in the confident figural style that distinguishes Nahl's best works. One of the miners has stopped work long enough to quench his thirst with water from a bucket. This has the effect of interrupting the implicit flow of time suggested by the action of the other workers and to inject a momentary pause for the observer's contemplation. This early mining scene subtly establishes, for the first time, a moralistic theme that reappears in many of Nahl's Gold Rush paintings and illustrations. It represents one of the popular American myths of the Gold Rush: that God's bounty in nature will reward the efforts of hard work shared among honest men, a sentiment offered to mitigate the self-serving motivation and lawless pursuits of many other Gold Rush participants.

After August Wenderoth married Nahl's half-sister Laura in 1856, the couple moved to

FIG. 44. Hugo Wilhelm Arthur Nahl, *The Fire in Sacramento,* 1852. Watercolor on paper, 4½ × 7⅛ in. Oakland Museum of California, gift of Concours d'Antiques, Art Guild.

Philadelphia. This vacancy in the studio prompted Charles to add Arthur to the family business that had been relocated to San Francisco in 1852 following the devastating fire in Sacramento. That same year Arthur Nahl produced a small watercolor *en grisaille* titled *The Fire in Sacramento,* 1852 (fig. 44). His little souvenir of the conflagration, rendered in a dramatically contrasting range of black and gray tones on white paper, may have been intended for reproduction in a publication. Nahl describes the historical fire in vivid detail. His tableau is populated with dozens of tiny figures shown beneath clouds of thick black smoke rising from the flaming buildings. In a frantic effort to stop the fire, a group of firefighters advances to the right side of the scene while crowds of people and horse-drawn wagons are rapidly moving toward the left in reckless retreat from the burning city.

Although a number of works survive that bear the signature of Arthur Nahl alone, more numerous were his collaborations with Charles. It seems that most of the Nahl brothers' early collaborative efforts were in portraiture. However, according to a letter from Arthur to his uncle Wilhelm in Germany telling him in 1854 of commissions to paint four panoramas, we conclude that he may also have been a competent landscape painter.

One such collaboration was on a scene titled *The Camp of a U.S. Coast Geodetic Survey Party* (fig. 45), painted in 1858. As part of a geodetic survey of the Pacific Coast, made in 1853 by the United States Department of Commerce, several artists had received commissions to produce images of topographical features for reproduction in government publications. Captain W. E. Greenwell, the man in charge of the survey between San Francisco and San Diego, also commissioned a series of six oil paintings from various artists, including the Nahls and the landscape painter Frederick A. Butman (see fig. 76), depicting the surveyors' camps in various locations.[4] The Nahl brothers' version, dated 1858, is particularly interesting as a rare example of their treatment of landscape. The camp, in an unspecified location, appears to be set up on an elevated plateau above the view of rolling hills seen below the horizon. The composition, in which most of the pictorial elements are parallel to the framing edges, is a less intricate composition than those used in most of the Nahls' genre subjects. The near-silhouette shapes of

FIG. 45. Charles Christian Nahl and Hugo Wilhelm Arthur Nahl, *The Camp of a U.S. Coast Geodetic Survey Party,* 1858. Oil on panel, 12½ × 18⅛ in. Collection of Santa Barbara Historical Society, Calif., gift of Mrs. Arthur Greenwell.

large oak trees, set against a luminous sky painted in gradations of warm yellow light on the left that shifts to clear azure blue on the right, provide the initial visual interest and effectively set a stage for the narrative. Verdant hillsides of spring are just beginning to take on the tawny golden tones of summer in California. The painting's immediate appeal as a landscape notwithstanding, the little vignettes of figures and animals set among the tents of the surveyors' campsite transform the work into a genre subject. This is consistent with the Nahls' preference for narrative content in all of their painting, except some portraits.

The Nahl brothers' observation of a day in the life of a surveyors' camp invites closer inspection of a number of pictorial details. The scene represents a temporary garrison during the apparent absence of the surveyors, who may be working in the field. Initial attention is drawn to the row of six white canvas tents located just below the center of the picture—their faceted shapes defined by strong sunlight and shadow. Closer inspection reveals such nearby details as a small flock of poultry, laundry drying on a clothesline, and a makeshift horse barn constructed of stacked hay bales. The large tent at the far right, with a projecting stovepipe, is probably the cook-tent and surveyors' mess. The American flag, flying from a tall flagpole at the far right edge of the painting, identifies the official, governmental nature of the depicted site and provides the picture's single note of bright color contrast. The observer's eye goes to the action at the lower center of the picture where the arrival of a man in wagon drawn by galloping white horses is announced by two, presumably barking, dogs at the front and rear. Nahl's reluctance to describe any scene devoid of incident is consistent with his stylistic inclination toward genre painting.

The most dramatic of the Nahl brothers' collaborative paintings is *Fire in San Francisco Bay* (fig. 46), a work that recreates an event in San Francisco's early history and gives Charles Christian Nahl, as the dominant artist, the opportunity to exercise his passion for history painting in a contemporary tableau. Nahl has depicted a battle scene in a style freely adapted from the famous military combats painted by his mentor, the renowned French painter and lithographer Horace Vernet. Charles had long admired the grandiose documentary battle scenes for which Vernet was so popular. As part of his own painting style, Nahl emulated Vernet's extensive use of anecdotal detail and the rendering of his subjects in a clear, descriptive light without obscuring selected passages in deep shadow. It is not known to what extent Arthur contributed to the finished work.

The depicted incident occurred on 24 May 1853, when two abandoned vessels converted to use as storage ships, the *Canonicus* and the *Manco,* caught fire in San Francisco harbor near the end of the Sacramento Street wharf. The primary factual sources of imagery in the painting were derived from a sketch drawn on top of a box by a grocer's delivery boy who had witnessed the conflagration.[5]

FIG. 46. Charles Christian Nahl and Hugo Wilhelm Arthur Nahl, *Fire in San Francisco Bay,* 1856. Oil on canvas, 26 × 40 in. Private collection.

The Nahl brothers' ambitious panoramic view of San Francisco that encompasses the eastern edge of the city, its harbor, and the burning ships side-by-side, was not completed until 1856. The scene is heavily populated with animated figures crowding the dockside and seen in rowboats pulling fire hoses through the water to firemen aboard the ships. Powder kegs on the *Manco* were prevented from exploding during a frenzied struggle to extinguish the flames. If the fire itself is not the real protagonist of the drama, it must then be the tiny figure of the fire chief who is standing between burning masts on the *Manco* directing the efforts of the waterfront fire brigade.

The dynamic composition is balanced asymmetrically with emphasis placed on the smoke and flames and their reflection in the water at the left-center foreground. This asymmetry belies the artists' use of a simple one-point perspective in which all the pictorial features are arranged along diagonal lines that radiate from a single vanishing point on the horizon—near the center of the painting. To enhance visual interest for the vast expanse of sky in the picture, Nahl divides the color between the left and right sides in gradations from blue to yellow as he did in his painting, *The Camp of a U.S. Geodetic Survey Party.* The imposing building shown in the distance is the United States Marine Hospital, then under construction.

From today's point of view, the painting could be seen as a work of pictorial journalism, but *Fire in San Francisco Bay* transcends mere illustration and becomes an example of a peculiarly American form of genre painting. In its straightforward, documentary style, this work does not express the political viewpoints or moralistic commentaries that characterize much European history painting. It makes its appeal to a new kind of art patronage on the American frontier, one with a taste for romantic realism.

From the mid-1850s through the late 1860s, Charles Christian Nahl turned again to the same idea of history and genre painting. Among these are a few small works on subjects that drew upon personal experiences that occurred during his family's arduous journey across Panama en route from New York to California. The Atlantic port of Chagres on the Isthmus was a picturesque tropical village that was also widely reputed to be a particularly dangerous and unhealthy environment for travelers. The romance of danger, the exotic flora and fauna of the tropics, and his contacts with the native culture made profound impressions on Nahl that were later incorporated into paintings done in his San Francisco studio.

Working from a series of detailed sketches that he made on the journey through the tropics, Nahl produced at least four paintings and several illustrations that deal with incidents that occurred on the trip across Panama. In letters to his family in Germany in 1852,[6] Charles discussed in detail the experiences of crossing the Isthmus that he later turned into subject matter for paintings such as *Chagres River*

FIG. 47. Charles Christian Nahl, *Chagres River Scene (Crossing the Chagres),* n.d. Oil on canvas mounted on board, 6¾ × 8⅞ in. Collection of Dr. Oscar and Trudy Lemer.

Scene (Crossing the Chagres) (fig. 47). The painting's focus of interest is a flat-bottomed bongo boat, crowded with passengers, as it is poled up the tranquil river. The sight of an overturned boat, snagged on treacherous rocks and floating debris, is the only reference to danger in an otherwise picturesque tropical landscape. Apparently, this small sketch is Nahl's preliminary study for a larger work titled *Incident on the Chagres River* (The Bancroft Library, University of California, Berkeley). The essential features of the landscape and boat remain the same, but the subject becomes significantly more dramatic with the depiction of a native falling overboard into a reputedly alligator-infested river.

Although Charles professed to be no landscape painter,[7] these small tropical scenes reveal his skill in rendering the essential features of a landscape to dramatic effect. Nahl's *Boaters Rowing to Shore at*

FIG. 48. Charles Christian Nahl, *Boaters Rowing to Shore at Chagres,* 1855. Oil on tin, 9¼ × 12 in. Collection of Dr. Oscar and Trudy Lemer.

Chagres, 1855 (fig. 48), is a very small painting that presents a predominantly landscape subject on a grand scale. It would, however, be uncharacteristic for Nahl to indulge in landscape for its own sake. He exercises his penchant for narrative historical content in a scene that uses topographical and architectural details to set a panoramic stage for a dramatic event.

Nahl takes an elevated viewpoint overlooking the scene in which the principal pictorial features, boats and waves, are arranged along opposing diagonal lines at the center foreground. The village of Chagres can be seen in the bright, hazy distance by the water's edge along the base of the hills at the right side of the painting. The ruins of an old Spanish fortress on top of a three-hundred-foot-high cliff, at the left of center, command a sweeping view of the river and the seaport of Chagres. Against this background, Nahl positions the small boatloads of disembarking steamship passengers who are being rowed, at their peril, through turbulent waves and among half-submerged timbers floating in the swells of the river—rendered in a translucent lime green.

Charles Nahl's exuberant color schemes were the subject of some harsh criticism during his own time. His frequent use of a dominant triad of high-key secondary hues (green, violet, and orange), or more often, the analogous tertiary hues (such as yellow green, blue green, red violet, red orange), contribute to the somewhat artificial look typical of Nahl's distinctive, bright color palette.

Notwithstanding a growing interest in paintings of historical subjects during the late 1850s, the mainstays of patronage for the busy Nahl studio in San Francisco continued to be portraiture and illustration. With the possible exception of the highly regarded William Smith Jewett, no other painter in

California enjoyed as large a patronage for portraits than Charles Christian Nahl. It has been suggested that the numerous commissions for portraits painted by Charles Nahl often required the assistance of his brother Arthur so that they could keep up with the demand. In 1858, Arthur wrote a letter to Wilhelm Nahl in Germany in which he described his role as a studio assistant to Charles: "We are working like a factory; Carl [Charles] paints the heads and I paint the garments."[8] This mass-production technique is blamed for stylistic inconsistencies and a certain lack of vitality found in some run-of the-mill portraits that bear the signature of C. Nahl. Many portraits were based on daguerreotypes, rather than on the more time-consuming multiple sittings by the subject, which would also account for the sheer volume of portraits emanating from the Nahl studio. Even so, when challenged or inspired by his subject, no other portrait painter in California surpassed the impeccable draftsmanship, precision of detail, or rendering of an extensive range of rich textures and lustrous surfaces that are evident in Nahl's best portraits. Of the more than fifty portraits of men, women, children, and families that have been documented as coming from the Nahl studio, many still exist and there may be many others yet to be located.

One subject where Charles excelled was in his portraits of children. An early and especially fine example is *Little Miss San Francisco,* 1853 (fig. 49). This utterly charming formal portrait of an otherwise unidentified little girl is a traditional studio set piece. She is carefully posed sitting on a chair inlaid with mother-of-pearl (which Nahl painted in reduced scale to suit the subject) that sits on a floral carpet in front of the requisite swag of fringed and tasseled drapery.

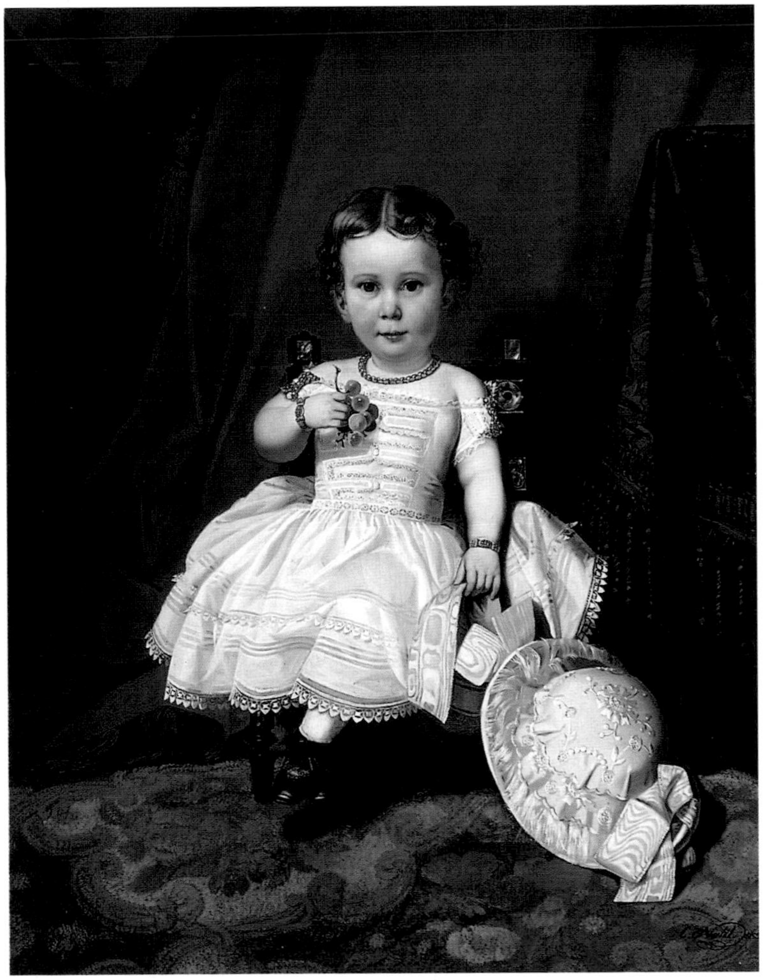

FIG. 49. Charles Christian Nahl, *Little Miss San Francisco,* 1853. Oil on canvas, 38 × 30 in. Crocker Art Museum, Sacramento, Calif., purchased with funds from Mrs. T. Warren Kyddson in memory of her husband, Dr. T. Warren Kyddson; Mr. and Mrs. Vern C. Jones; Crocker Art Museum Association Memorial Funds; and others.

FIG. 50. Charles Christian Nahl, *Portrait of Jane Eliza Steen Johnson,* 1858. Oil on canvas, 34¼ × 26½ in. Oakland Museum of California, gift of Dr. Gerald H. Gray.

The artist has captured the essential qualities of youthful innocence and vitality—a daunting challenge to most portrait painters—that conveys a convincing truth of the likeness. The child wears a crisp white dress lavishly trimmed with delicate lace. In her right hand she grasps a small bunch of green grapes and in the other she holds the white moiré satin ribbon attached to a fancy, pale yellow hat. Nahl took obvious pleasure in rendering the particular details and textures of embroidery and ostrich feathers on the elaborately decorated hat. The continuity of technique and the consistently high quality of detail in this painting leave little doubt of its attribution to the hand of Charles Nahl alone.

FIG. 51. Jean-Auguste-Dominique Ingres, *Madame Moitessier,* 1851. Oil on canvas, 69½ × 51¾ in. National Gallery of Art, Washington, D.C., Samuel H. Kress collection. Board of Trustees, National Gallery of Art, Washington, D.C.

Of exceptional quality is Charles Nahl's *Portrait of Jane Eliza Steen Johnson* (fig. 50). The elegant three-quarter-length formal portrait of a San Francisco lady painted in 1858 is reminiscent, in style and fashion, of Jean-Auguste-Dominique Ingres's portrait, *Madame Moitessier* (fig. 51), painted in 1851. Although it seems unlikely that Nahl could have known about the Ingres after coming to America in 1849, the painting is representative of a formula for society portraits in the classical style that was popular in France when Nahl studied in Paris. Common to both portraits are the sitter's characteristic direct gaze at the observer, the impeccably smoothed hairline framing the face, the bared shoulders, the black velvet and lace gown, and the comparable fashion accessories that are the embodiment of material grace and wealth requisite to the mode. Nahl's academic training is apparent in the exquisite draftsmanship and high degree of finish that give a full measure of attention to every high-fashion detail.

Jane Eliza Steen Johnson and her husband arrived in San Francisco from Ireland during the Gold Rush. They opened a dry-goods and millinery store called the Lace House on Sacramento Street near Portsmouth Square. There the attractive, high-spirited Jane Eliza modeled clothing and other finery for the miners to buy as gifts for their wives or girlfriends.[9] This splendid, formal portrait depicts Jane Eliza luxuriously dressed in a black velvet Parisian ball gown corseted and elaborately trimmed with fine black lace, and wearing a blue satin ribbon in her hair. She holds a folded cockade fan with ostrich feathers and ivory handle, and has adorned herself with jeweled gold rings, bracelets, earrings, a pendant cross, and a brooch set with a daguerreotype portrait of her son. Overall, Nahl's opulent portrait, notwithstanding the remarkable likeness confirmed by an earlier daguerreotype, also to some extent constitutes an advertisement for The Lace House emporium.

Charles Christian Nahl's talent for drawing and painting the human figure with anatomical accuracy and realistic animation is evident in his prodigious output of genre subjects for illustrations as well as paintings. Another manifestation of his interest in human anatomy was his regular regime of physical culture, undertaken with his brother, Arthur, and like-minded friends. They founded the first athletic club in America, and even wrote a book on the subject.

During the 1860s the Nahl brothers remained active, individually and collaboratively, producing graphic designs and illustrations. Decoratively illustrated certificates and diplomas were commissioned for members of various civic and fraternal organizations. Charles also designed special commemorative pictorials suitable for framing, such as his memorial to Abraham Lincoln, that were lithographed for distribution to subscribers, and he worked as an illustrator of anecdotal historical incidents that frequently drew upon Gold Rush lore and were published to accompany poetry, short stories, and books by various authors. It was the Nahl brothers' prolific illustrations of life in the mines, appearing in many widely distributed publications from the early days of the Gold Rush, that were responsible for giving the world its most enduring images of the Forty-niner.

The millionaire merchant, railroad, and banking tycoons who prospered from the Gold Rush and Silver Bonanza became California's aristocracy. As the wealthy members of the San Francisco and Sacramento elite indulged their fondness for foreign travel, with the de rigueur Continental Grand Tour, they soon acquired a taste for collecting European art to complement their cultural aspirations. This shift in preference caused much harm to the local art market. As more and more Italian, French, and German painting and sculpture was brought from Europe, many fine California artists complained of a severe drop in their commissions and sales.

Charles Nahl was one of only a few local painters who achieved a comfortable measure of success in the 1860s and 1870s with commissions for paintings in the European style. Subjects drawn from history, literature, and classical mythology graced the lavishly furnished mansions of prominent families, among them the Stanfords, Floods, Bests, and Crockers. Charles Nahl's most devoted patron was Judge Edwin Bryant Crocker of Sacramento, who was also a collector of European paintings and fine old-master drawings. Under Judge Crocker's patronage, Nahl received the opportunity to indulge his longtime interest in painting the romantic and neoclassical subjects that he had studied in European prototypes during his formative years. Among his forays into the romantic style are three equestrian works inspired by Théodore Géricault and Eugène Delacroix, *Joaquin Murietta,* 1868 (private collection), Nahl's sensational depiction of the legendary California bandit; *The Love Chase,* 1869, a somewhat sentimental Arabian fantasy; and its pendant work (both are in the Crocker Art Museum, Sacramento, California), *The Patriotic Race,* 1870, with related imagery adapted to an American Revolutionary theme.

Nahl followed these works with a trilogy of paintings for Crocker based on the legend of the Romans and the Sabine women. This series provided the artist with the freedom to demonstrate his competence as an academic classicist in a style influenced by the great French masters Nicolas Poussin and Jean-Auguste-Dominique Ingres. The commission enabled Nahl to display his highly disciplined technique in representing such pictorial details as complex figure groupings in action poses—without benefit of live models—voluptuous translucent flesh tones, and the skillful handling of drapery folds and textures. But Nahl's distinctive, high-keyed color palette and polished surfaces, although still much admired, were already somewhat out of style at the time.[10]

FIG. 52. Charles Christian Nahl, *Fandango,* 1873. Oil on canvas, 72 × 108 in. Crocker Art Museum, Sacramento, Calif., E. B. Crocker Collection.

In 1873, Charles Nahl followed his masterpiece, *Sunday Morning in the Mines* (see fig. 81), with a companion piece, *Fandango* (fig. 52), also commissioned by Crocker, that illustrates life in the days of the Spanish rancho period in California. Although *Fandango* has an equally theatrical subject with multiple figures, including dancers and equestrian riders, the depicted celebration is without obvious moral implications.

Charles Nahl and, perhaps to a lesser extent, Arthur Nahl enjoyed their well-respected reputations and popularity until the ends of their lives. Toward the end of the nineteenth century, however, as artistic styles were changing, public interest in the Nahl brothers' paintings, and other manifestations of Victorian taste, declined. It is for their Gold Rush paintings and drawings in particular that they should be long remembered.

Fig. 53. Ernest Narjot, *Placer Operations at Foster's Bar,* 1851. Oil on panel, 12 × 14 in. The Bancroft Library, University of California, Berkeley.

Souvenirs of the Mother Lode

ERNEST NARJOT AND GEORGE HENRY BURGESS

Harvey L. Jones

THE PROFESSIONAL LIFE OF ERNEST NARJOT, a pioneer California artist, spanned nearly a half century beginning with his arrival in San Francisco during the early years of the Gold Rush. Ernest Etienne Narjot de Francheville was born on Christmas Day, 1826, to a French family of artists in Brittany. He had received his early art training from his parents and continued his studies at an art school in Paris before the age of sixteen. An adventurous young man, Narjot yielded to the temptation of riches in faraway California. He set sail from France and endured the rigors of the voyage around Cape Horn, arriving in San Francisco sometime between 1849 and 1851 to join the throng of prospectors headed for the goldfields.[1]

Although Narjot had little success as a miner, he drew upon his art training to turn his observations and experiences from the diggings into subjects for paintings. Among his earliest paintings that deal with a mining theme is *Placer Operations at Foster's Bar,* 1851 (fig. 53). Narjot's apparent fascination with the technical aspects of placer mining gives this painting its documentary character. The wealth of descriptive details of the entire operation indicates that the artist's observations were sketched on site. Borthwick described Foster's Bar as "a place about half a mile long, with the appearance of having slipped down off the face of the mountains, and thus formed a flat along the side of the [Yuba] river."[2]

Because placer mining had become a group activity in the interest of efficiency, various mechanical devices were increasingly used for greater control over the watercourses. Narjot's painting depicts a mining camp occupied by eight or ten men beside a mountain stream where a dam is under construction, trenches being dug, and waterwheels used to collect and divert the flow of water for the recovery of gold. Narjot's wooded landscape surrounding the operation, disturbed by the presence of tents, felled trees, a dam, excavations, and elaborate wooden structures, shows the miners' immediate and harsh impact on the environment. The figure dressed in a red jacket and shown leaning on a large rock in the center foreground of the painting represents a Native American's poignant observation of this apparent exploitation of nature. Narjot's composition for this painting, depicting the man-made angular forms in a criss-cross linear arrangement that overlays the natural contours of the landscape, further underscores the miners' destructiveness.

Failing to find success in California either as a miner or as an artist, Narjot moved to Mexico, where for several years he worked the mines and painted. In the late 1860s he was back in California and established in a studio on Clay Street in San Francisco, where he accepted commissions for portraits, landscapes, and genre scenes, as well as frescoes for murals in churches and public buildings.

Influenced by the French school of his early academic training, Narjot's mature paintings revealed their stylistic sources in his choice of traditional subject matter rendered in somewhat idealized, romantic terms (see figs. 84, 85, and 86). He was attracted to imaginative subjects drawn from literature— such as his portrayal of the sacrifice of a Druid priestess. More popular were Narjot's picturesque genre scenes of ethnic subjects that were not based upon reality but on romanticized concepts of frontier life among the Indians, the Mexicans, or the urban Chinese in San Francisco. These he continued painting throughout the 1880s and he enjoyed the recognition of his profession with awards for exhibited paintings and commissions for new public works.

A contemporary of Narjot whose artistic life in California spanned a comparable period is George Henry Burgess. Many of Burgess's paintings are steeped in the colorful daily life of the Gold Rush years. From his initial attempts in the 1850s to strike it rich as a prospector to as late as the 1890s, when he was a well-established artist in San Francisco, he seemed preoccupied with the images and events surrounding the discovery of gold in California. He was one of four sons of a prominent physician in London. The eldest brother, Edward, was the first to reach California in 1847 as a member of Colonel Jonathan D. Stevenson's California Regiment sent to occupy San Francisco harbor during the Mexican War. Edward remained in San Francisco, where he maintained a lucrative trading business between California and the Hawaiian Islands. Hubert, a multifaceted Argonaut—artist, jeweler, teacher, hunter, and inventor—set out by ship for California in 1850 after the news of the great discovery reached him in New York. Charles and George, crossing the plains sometime in 1850, joined the other Burgess brothers in their quest for California gold.

Soon, however, George, Hubert, and Charles turned from pick and pan to open their own small jewelry shop. Working out of a tent in Sonora, the brothers impressed their fellow miners by repairing watches and fashioning rings and chains out of the precious metal brought in from local diggings.

Sometime in 1850, jealous Americans levied a tax on foreign miners and proceeded to drive the Mexicans, Chilenos, and Frenchmen out of the Sonora area. According to Hubert, enraged Americans and Mexicans clashed and the resulting violence effectively destroyed many small business enterprises. Fearful of being robbed of their rings and watches, the brothers decided to leave Sonora and go their own way.[3]

Many Forty-niners who had limited success as prospectors were forced to seek alternative means of support. Hubert Burgess supplemented his income as a professional hunter, providing meat for

FIG. 54. George Henry Burgess, *Hunters in the Gold Country,* n.d. Oil on canvas, 8 ¼ × 11 ⅞ in. Collection of Dr. Oscar and Trudy Lemer.

miners' tables in boardinghouses and restaurants in Gold Rush towns and cities. Hubert had instilled in his brother George an appreciation for the outdoor life—especially an enthusiasm for hunting small game. Their travels together on foot or on horseback while hunting in the gold country yielded many small sketches and paintings that artfully document a life away from the diggings. For *Hunters in the Gold Country* (fig. 54), George Burgess painted what appears to be an autobiographical depiction, himself and Hubert on one of their hunting expeditions. This small oil on canvas reveals the artist's pleasure in a scene that conveys both the grandeur of the mountain landscape and a personal expression of intimacy with nature. The anecdotal subject, the two hunters on a forest trail, places it within the genre category. This "cabinet-size" painting, a nineteenth-century term used to describe small easel pictures on canvas executed in the artist's studio, was probably developed from a field sketch on paper.

In another work related to his hunting experiences, George Burgess has carefully composed a mountain landscape vignette within a vertical oval format. The small, untitled, undated watercolor of a

FIG. 55. George Henry Burgess, Untitled (man crossing a stream), n.d. Watercolor on paper, 6 × 4½ in. The Bancroft Library, University of California, Berkeley.

FIG. 56. George Henry Burgess, *Miners Working Beside a Stream,* n.d. Watercolor on paper, 6⅞ × 5 in. Collection of Dr. Oscar and Trudy Lemer.

man crossing a stream (fig. 55) depicts the hunter on horseback shouldering a rifle as he pauses in midstream to allow his mount to drink. A certain emphasis on the figure aside, it is in the delicate rendering of foliage and topography in a rhythmic arrangement of soft, curvilinear contours, with gleaming reflections on the gently flowing stream, that this tranquil scene makes its decorative appeal to Victorian taste. Hubert Burgess expresses an appreciation of the beauty of such a California landscape while lamenting gold mining's damage to the environment:

> The country is rapidly changing here in appearance. California is remarkable for the splendors of its autumnal colors. The foliage is now to be seen in all the possible shades of green and brown. The surface of the rocks likewise changes color, the mosses alike clinging to them, altering their shades. George and I, in going down the M[okelumne] River, were several times stopped by the grandeur of the scenery. The only drawback to the view is the color of the water. So much work being done up the rivers, its color is brown instead of as I have seen it, clear as crystal. The salmon still pass up but to certain death. . . . [4]

George's idealized depictions of a pristine California landscape avoid any indications of environmental pollution that would certainly compromise the painting's artistic merit for a nineteenth-century art collector.

In his drawings and watercolors, particularly those where the landscape is a dominant feature, George Burgess employs a delicate, lyrical approach to the artful composition with a careful attention to chiaroscuro that reflects his academic training. *Miners Working Beside a Stream,* n.d. (fig. 56), a monochromatic watercolor highlighted with white, is an example of the artist's ability to develop his subject almost entirely by massing areas of contrasting values, without resorting to the use of outline or color. The painting virtually

FIG. 57. George Henry Burgess, *Artist's Gold Mining Camp,* 1854. Watercolor on board, 4⅞ × 7¾ in. Collection of Dr. Oscar and Trudy Lemer.

succeeds as pure landscape, its deftly rendered patches of sunlight and shadow describing a waterfall in a woodland interior with an aesthetic appeal that almost makes the group of miners in the foreground seem merely incidental.

Burgess leaves a remembrance of his prospecting days in a watercolor, *Artist's Gold Mining Camp,* 1854 (fig. 57). In this affectionate view of his campsite, he depicts a small tent pitched beneath the dense foliage of a low-branching tree on a hillside. A small dog waits outside the tent where a man is seen sitting in the dark interior while another is shown carrying a bucket as he walks toward a nearby stream—on the other side of which a figure waves from the doorway of another tent. The back of the picture bears a partly illegible inscription in the hand of the artist:

> Tent where Charles [a brother] and I camped in 1854, back of Butte City Mountain, rich dry . . . had been found near by—We sunk a shaft through hard cement but although near the fortunate ones—found nothing. I picked up some pieces of gold while drinking of a spring near our camp. Charles went back to Butte City, I remained in the tent for a few days.

In his views of towns and mining scenes, Burgess relies upon observed factual data for their illustrative value, and pays less attention to the romantic idiom. This firsthand familiarity with the sites and activities of the mining regions informs Burgess's drawings and watercolors with their authenticity of detail. Being in the goldfields, George was able to describe the fascinating mechanics of recovering gold and to develop a fresh approach to the pictorial opportunities afforded the sensitive artist. His straightforward visual descriptions were sketched on the spot, usually in pencil or pen and ink on paper, sometimes with the addition of watercolor —media that artists favor for efficiency and convenience.

By 1850, as greater numbers of miners were staking claims on the land, it was necessary to dig further up in the hills away from convenient sources of the water needed to wash out the gold. Burgess's watercolor titled *Mining at Tunnel Hill, Jackson, Amador County, California,* 1853 (fig. 58), illustrates a team of miners at work using a trestle structure to transport ore cars, loaded with rocks dug from a tunnel on the hillside, that are sent down to be dumped into the valley below for further processing. The picturesque landscape setting does little to mitigate the clearly apparent harsh reality of hard labor expressed by the hot sun beating down on gritty rock piles and the bent back of the miner who is pushing an ore car along the trestle. This is a work that might have appealed to miners rather than to art collectors of the period.

George Burgess's extensive travels throughout the gold country yielded wide-ranging opportunities for varied subject matter for paintings. His small watercolor, *Mother Lode Inn,* n.d. (fig. 59), is a genre painting that makes some fascinating observations touching upon the larger implication of the effect of the Gold Rush on California's future. Burgess has offered a glimpse into the encroachment of the Gold Rush upon land that is neither town nor mining camp. This wayside inn for travelers is depicted at the junction of two well-established trails at an unspecified location. The major compositional elements are arranged parallel to the roadways that converge at the center of the painting in the middle distance. On either side of the big tree that anchors this composition at the center are several permanent structures including the eponymous lodging. Activities such as the big log being hauled in by oxcart, the hay wagon, the rail fence enclosure, and the presence of a few attendant personnel at the inn, all illustrate the invasion of the natural landscape. It is, however, the juxtaposition of this scene with the family of dark-skinned Native Americans and their black dog, shown almost in silhouette in the center foreground, that expresses the most poignant implication of this settlement. The apparent symbolic confrontation between the black dog and the resident white dog reveals the subtext for this otherwise innocent genre scene.

In 1853, at the urgings of Edward, whose trading business with the islands afforded George and

FIG. 58. George Henry Burgess, *Mining at Tunnel Hill, Jackson, Amador County, California,* 1853. Watercolor on paper, 6¾ × 10⅛ in. Sacramento Archives & Museum Collection Center, Calif., Eleanor McClatchy Collection.

FIG. 59. George Henry Burgess, *Mother Lode Inn,* n.d. Watercolor on paper, 5 × 8¾ in. Louis A. Capellino.

his brothers an escape from their rugged living conditions in California, they went to live among the natives in Hawaii's balmy climate. Charles worked as a paperhanger, Hubert prospered in the jewelry business, receiving commissions from the Hawaiian monarch King Kamehameha. Meanwhile, George painted a number of watercolors and made drawings on stone in preparation for lithographed views of Hawaii. *Port of Honolulu* (printed in 1857) was typical of his stylistic preference for accurate yet simplified descriptive details for specific buildings and various types of vessels in a scene populated with active figures drawn to scale. This work bears the printed inscriptions: "Drawn from nature on stone by G. H. Burgess" and "Printed by Britton and Rey"—a prominent firm of lithographers in San Francisco. His scenes depicting the Hawaiian peoples, the figure groups composed in the manner of academic European exemplars, show the artist in a more romantic vein.

After less than two years in the islands, apparently rejuvenated by their tranquil sojourn, the Burgess brothers returned to the vicissitudes of life in California. George soon became disillusioned with lithography. In letters to his mother in England, he wrote about his continuing quarrels with the owners and other employees at Britton and Rey over their assertions about the excessive amount of time he was taking for his drawings on the lithographic stones. Further disagreement ensued over the credits given to a minor collaborator, instead of to Burgess himself, as the principal draftsman in some of the published lithographs.[5] George Burgess gave up lithography in favor of less collaborative forms of art that would allow him greater freedom of choice.

Settling in San Francisco after returning from Hawaii, Burgess established a studio and embarked on a career as a professional artist. In the 1855 San Francisco directory, he is listed as an engraver on wood at 121 Pine Street. Few examples of wood engraving attributed to Burgess are known today. Portrait commissions formed the bulk of his livelihood during the next two decades as an art patronage began to develop among the city's wealthy and socially ambitious winners of the Gold Rush. His portraits were praised for the skill with which he rendered delicate lace on the ladies' gowns. Burgess would have the subject of his portrait bring her fancy gown to his studio several days in advance of her sitting so that he could take more time to paint its decorative details.[6] He was also in demand by photo galleries, to handpaint photographic portraits—a popular, affordable alternative to the more expensive traditional painted portraiture. Burgess was among the first artists to paint the scenic wonders of Yosemite in the late 1850s, but it is for the Gold Rush genre scenes that he is best remembered.

There were few opportunities for Burgess to exhibit his paintings publicly during the 1850s. The local Mechanics' Institute did not hold exhibitions until 1857; Burgess showed portraits that year and watercolor landscapes in the 1858 exhibition.[7] After two attempts in the 1860s to establish a viable artists'

FIG. 60. George Henry Burgess, *San Francisco in July, 1849,* 1891. Oil on canvas, 62 × 143 in. Oakland Museum of California, gift of the Women's Board.

association had failed, a group of prominent citizens, art patrons, and local artists, including George Burgess, founded the San Francisco Art Association in 1871. This was the beginning of regular exhibitions and patronage for the arts in California.

In 1877 George Burgess was commissioned to paint a full-length portrait of James Clair Flood, a Forty-niner saloon keeper who later made his fortune in silver from the Comstock Lode. Flood built a monumental and ornate Victorian house called Linden Towers in the San Francisco suburb of Menlo Park, as well as the splendid mansion atop Nob Hill that survives today (renovated after the fire of 1906) as the home of the Pacific Union Club.[8] It is not known if this portrait still exists. However, the painting that Flood commissioned from the artist in 1878, *View of San Francisco in 1850* (see fig. 87), remains as an important record of San Francisco's early history. It is presumed that Flood had ordered this comprehensive view of "old" San Francisco for the newly completed Linden Towers. Burgess was paid $650 for the painting and an additional $100 for the frame.

As the port of entry for Gold Rush prospectors, San Francisco experienced a phenomenal surge of growth in a matter of months following news of the discovery of gold in California. By the fall of 1849, the population of the city had grown from about eight hundred to thirty-five thousand. During this period, a number of artists executed panoramic views of the city in drawings, watercolors, or paintings that served various purposes. Some drawings were reproduced on letter sheets that provided the miners with an illustration to accompany correspondence back home. Lithographic prints and book illustrations offered images of the fabled San Francisco that could be disseminated throughout the world cheaply. The paintings on canvas seemed to serve a higher artistic purpose that corresponds to the long-established tradition of history painting.

For George Burgess, a nostalgic look back from the 1880s also produced a painting titled *San Francisco in July, 1849* (fig. 60) that would become the culminating experience of his professional life. Some time after 1891, Burgess himself prophesied: "That this picture is destined to reach the highest value, which any painting could have for this city or state, is evident. It is the infant village put before us, from which our great city has emerged."[9]

George Burgess began work on his magnum opus in 1882. Over the next four years he was constantly involved with the research and preparation of this painstakingly accurate representation of San Francisco as it had appeared in the year before he himself had first seen it. A watercolor triptych made by William Birch McMurtrie in 1849 (see fig. 17 for part of it) was the source of the view and of many of the pictorial features of his great panorama. Burgess also consulted existing contemporary sketches, daguerreotypes, and lithographic views for confirmation of various topographical and structural details.

In his obsession for unassailable authenticity, Burgess sought to verify the factual aspects of the painting with testimonials signed by more than two hundred eyewitnesses who had been pioneers. They included two governors, a mayor, a former alcalde, and dozens of other prominent San Franciscans, some of whom had arrived before 1849.[10] Burgess himself described the scene:

> The visitor to San Francisco [circa 1890] would scarcely believe . . . that the brushy hill in the foreground of the picture is where the stock exchange now stands, and the sandy rises to the left where are the two horsemen is now Montgomery and Pine. The hill Lloma [*sic*] Alta of General Vallejo's time, in the middle distance, is Telegraph Hill, from whence, for many years after the date of the picture, ships were signaled to the merchants of the little town, as they entered the Golden Gate. Between it and Russian Hill, the national flag flies over the Plaza, on which the red tiled adobe was used as the Custom House. In the foreground . . . corner of Montgomery and California was the Leidesdorff Cottage, which at the date of the picture was occupied by Captain George Stoneman (afterwards our Governor) who had charge of our city's gold. . . . Some of the hundreds of vessels seen in the harbor, are unable to get away for want of seamen. . . . up the Clay Street Hill is the Post Office with its long file of applicants for letters.[11]

He had almost completed the scene by 1886 when he began his prolonged quest for a buyer. By the time it was finished (the copyright date is 1891), Burgess was wanting to sell the painting for ten thousand dollars. His repeated attempts to sell the canvas at that price met with failure—perhaps because it was painted so many years after the fact. In 1894 Burgess signed over his copyright to Elisha Cook of the

H. S. Crocker Company of San Francisco to produce a chromolithograph of the scene. Eventually Burgess relinquished his control of the painting for a loan of two thousand dollars in gold on the condition that, if a buyer could be found at a higher price, he would repay the lender with interest. However, the artist was unable to make repayment and he lost the painting by foreclosure in 1897.[12]

George Burgess found his longtime efforts to create this historic panorama, *San Francisco in July, 1849*, and his failure to sell it, to be the most frustrating and disappointing experiences of his professional life. It is ironic that the painting, now in the permanent collection of the Oakland Museum of California, is the work by which the artist is best remembered today.

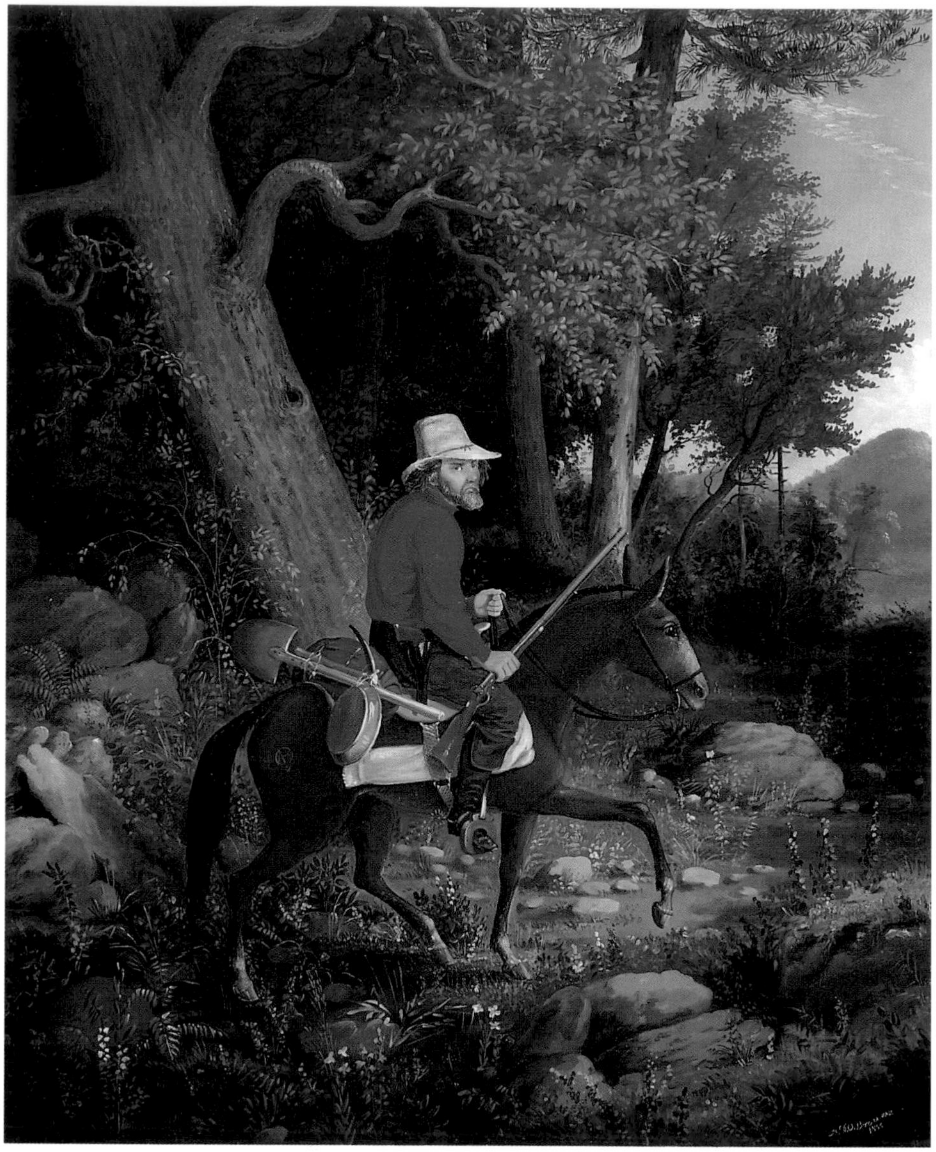

FIG. 61. A. D. O. Browere, *The Lone Prospector,* 1853. Oil on canvas, 50 × 30 in. Oakland Museum of Calfornia, on extended loan from Hideko Goto Packard.

Mining the Picturesque

A. D. O. BROWERE

Janice T. Driesbach

A LATECOMER TO CALIFORNIA, the New York artist A. D. O. Browere arrived in 1852, after a four-month voyage via Cape Horn. Browere's first trip to the Pacific coincided with what is considered to be the last years of the Gold Rush, and although would-be miners would arrive for many years, claims were harder to establish and gold more difficult to acquire. Browere's motives for venturing to California are uncertain; like many other Argonauts, he had achieved some stature in the East (the trip was, after all, costly), but his accomplishments were modest. If he traveled to California for gold, there is little evidence that he worked any claims; if he was seeking prosperity as an artist, he seems to have made little effort to market his paintings to his most likely audience—the newly affluent residents of San Francisco and the mining communities.

The son of a sculptor, Browere exhibited scenes from *Rip Van Winkle* at the National Academy of Design during the 1830s, and earned an award in 1841 for his *Canonicus and the Governor of Plymouth.* After that time, however, he was only sporadically represented in National Academy exhibitions, generally with historical canvases. Although the artist moved to Catskill—a site made famous by artists of the Hudson River school—in 1834, he listed his address as Brooklyn in 1844, indicating that he maintained close connections with New York City until at least the mid-1840s.[1] In Catskill, a view of which (fig. 62) he painted in 1849, Browere evidently struggled to support his growing family. Employed as a clerk in a drugstore and as a carriage and sign painter, he seemed to have little time for his own painting.[2]

FIG. 62. A. D. O. Browere, *Catskill, New York,* 1849. Oil on canvas, 34 × 44 in. Brooklyn Museum of Art, Dick S. Ramsay Fund. 40.881

The promise of wealth may have been the impetus for Browere's first trip West, and it was long assumed that he headed directly to the mines after arriving in California. A listing for "J. D. Brower," carriage painter, in the 1852 San Francisco city directory suggests, however, that the artist settled there for some time. He probably did

FIG. 63. A. D. O. Browere, *Miner's Return,* 1854. Oil on canvas, 24 × 30 in. Collection of Everett Millard.

so to earn sufficient money to purchase the costly supplies needed for a journey to the mines.[3] Once he was able, Browere seems to have departed for the Sierra foothills.

Because Browere made two trips to California (between 1852 and 1856 and again from 1858 to 1861) and many of his paintings are undated, it is difficult to determine a definitive chronology for his Gold Rush subjects.[4] His first documented California painting, *The Lone Prospector* (fig. 61), of 1853, is a variation on a contemporary local model—*A Miner Prospecting* by Charles Christian Nahl and August Wenderoth. Browere most likely met Nahl while he was in San Francisco, and saw *A Miner Prospecting* there. If not, he knew it from the lithographs that Nahl and Wenderoth made, some of which were hand colored.

Although the central figure, with its outsize head and right foot clumsily placed into the stirrup, is awkwardly drawn, *The Lone Prospector* is one of Browere's most engaging figure paintings. The artist closely followed Nahl's prototype, and the variety and clarity of the flowers in the foreground shows the artist's interest in horticulture.[5] Browere's interpretation differs from the earlier *Miner Prospecting* in that Nahl's Forty-niner is mounted on a handsome white horse leading a pack mule. He has a knife inside his boot and a large bedroll rather than a pick and shovel. In contrast, *The Lone Prospector* is astride a mule, which is branded with the artist's initials. Whereas Nahl's figure appears to glare out at the viewer, Browere's miner averts his eyes. Despite the absence of any identifiable immediate threat, *The Lone Prospector* appears wary, reluctant to proceed. His discomfort amidst the verdant landscape sets Browere's miner apart from Nahl's, and likewise distinguishes him from contemporaneous representations of mountain men in the West by artists such as Charles Deas and W. F. Tait.[6]

By the summer of 1854, Browere settled in Columbia, in the center of California's southern mining region. With a colleague, he purchased a house at the rear of the American Baking Company and advertised a "sign and ornamental painting office."[7] Even though he had decided to set himself up in business in California, Browere's *Miner's Return* (fig. 63), painted that year, suggests that he was profoundly lonely at this time. According to family tradition, the composition shows the artist's return to Catskill, New York. However, it was painted two years before he went home, so the emotional scene must represent a joyous moment Browere imagined. Here a miner (reputedly a self-portrait) embraces his wife while his daughters and mother rush from the cabin to greet him. The gentleman at the right who looks heavenward and clasps his hands in prayer of thanks for the miner's safe return has been identified as Browere's uncle, Solomon Davis.[8] Significantly, Browere depicted the culminating episode of the miner's adventure in a manner similar to his earlier scenes from *Rip Van Winkle,* with figures clustered in a shallow foreground space that forms a stage for the action. In both this compositional format and his stylized rendering of emotions, Browere adapted approaches from the Düsseldorf school of painting, which would have been familiar to him from the attention being accorded Emanuel Leutze's work and exhibitions that had been on view in New York since 1850. His use of academic conventions rather than direct observation in developing his narrative canvases reflects Browere's reliance on models to compose his paintings. As the figures in *Miner's Return* were people close to Browere, the artist may have made the composition for his own enjoyment. He does not, however, seem to have exhibited his work in California, nor to have realized many sales. In fact, he apparently took most of his paintings back East following his first stay in the mines.[9]

FIG. 64. A. D. O. Browere, *John C. Duchow, Jr.*, ca. 1855. Oil on canvas, 30 × 25 in. California Historical Society, San Francisco, gift of Warren R. Howell.

Browere did secure a patron in John C. Duchow Jr., the founder and publisher of the *Columbia Gazette,* who commissioned Browere to paint a mining scene, and subsequently ordered portraits of himself and of his parents. *John C. Duchow, Jr.* (fig. 64) is a stiff representation of its subject; surely Browere was more comfortable painting genre scenes and landscapes. Indeed, in contrast, his *Miners of Placerville* (fig. 65), also painted at this time, is an engaging composition that offers considerable detail as well as insights into a number of mining operations.

Although miners continued to work in Columbia into the 1860s, Browere's complex painting represents activities more characteristic of the early years of the Gold Rush, when gold was more readily accessible. Browere illustrates many kinds of mining in this canvas; at the center foreground, a miner is panning, at the left, another is working with a pick ax. In the right middle ground, two men are felling a large tree for wood to construct either rockers and long toms or more housing.[10] The canvas-covered cabins in the background were prevalent at southern mining sites. Browere conveys the frenzied activity that pervaded mining camps, and acknowledges the necessity for miners to form partnerships to divert rivers and operate equipment, developments that were occurring when he was observing such scenes.

Most likely also dating from this time is *Prospectors in the Sierra* (fig. 66), one of a number of enchanting landscapes that Browere enlivened with the presence of incidental figures. These compositions show how California's distinctive geography impressed the artist, and document the appearance of

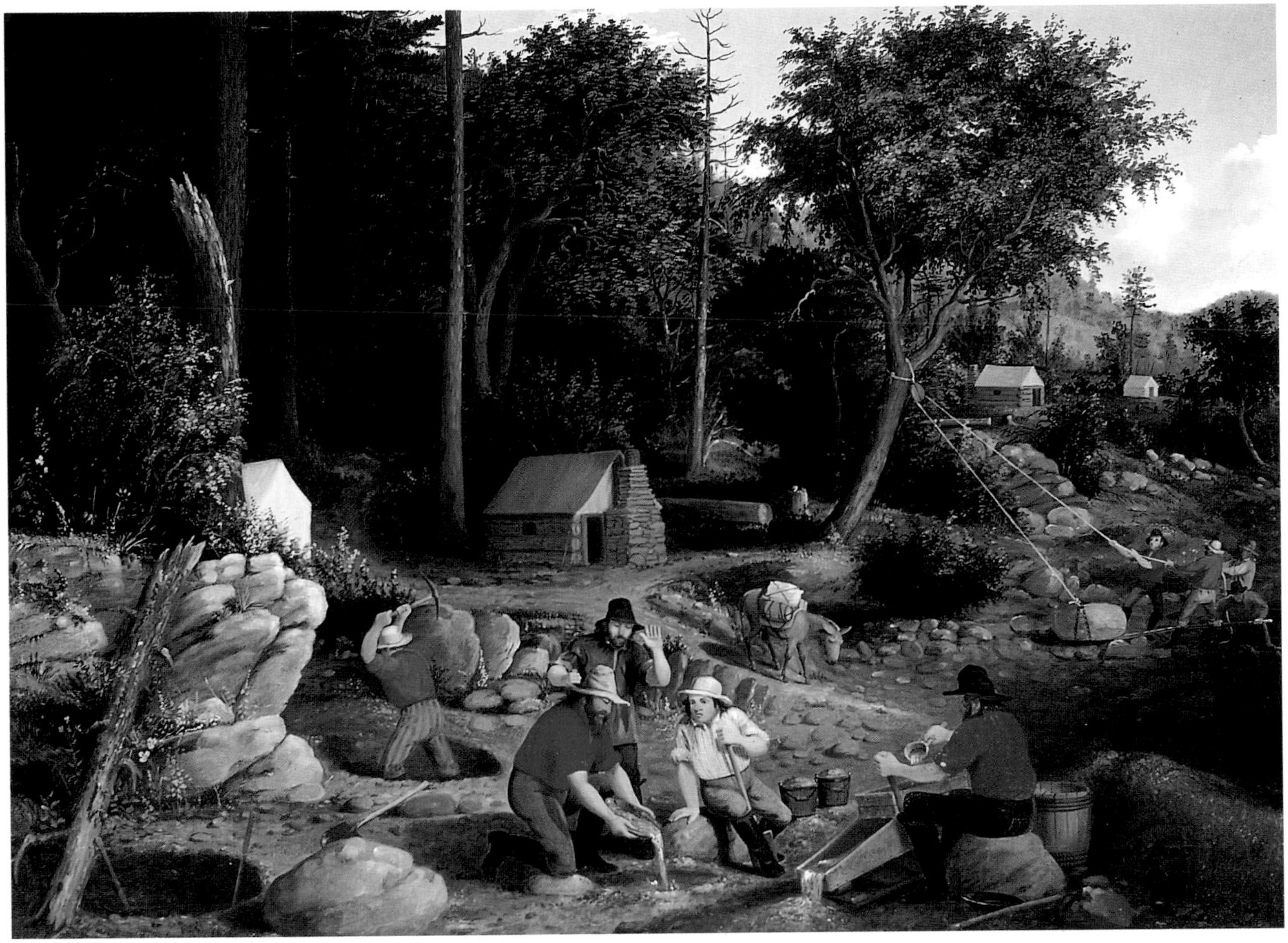

FIG. 65. A. D. O. Browere, *Miners of Placerville,* 1855. Oil on canvas, 26 × 36 in. National Cowboy Hall of Fame and Western Heritage Center, Oklahoma City, Oklahoma.

FIG. 66. A. D. O. Browere, *Prospectors in the Sierra,* ca. 1854. Oil on canvas, 35 × 60 in. F. E. Keeler III.

the Sierra foothills during the Gold Rush era.[11] They are larger than the artist's earlier landscapes and in each case, having been painted "at a very unspecific time of day," suggest that his primary interest was in recording the singular topography rather than in capturing dramatic lighting effects.[12]

Also associated with Browere's first journey to California is *Jamestown or D. O. Mills' Mill* (fig. 67). This painting, which may date to the mid-1850s, offers an idyllic landscape, the mill being set far into the distance alongside a river. In fact, a driver seated high on a hay wagon is more prominent, giving the subject a rural character uncommon in Browere's work. The tenderly rendered scene shows similarities with contemporary British landscape painting, and—from the treatment of the branch overhanging the water—may be unfinished.[13]

Browere also painted the first, and possibly the second, of three versions of a view of Stockton during his first journey to California. Why he created three nearly identical scenes of this thriving trading center for mining communities along the tributaries of the San Joaquin River is not known. An inscription on the latest of the paintings (1858, Haggin Museum, Stockton) testifies that Browere was working "from a sketch painted on the spot," and the composition is unique in Browere's oeuvre in featuring identifiable buildings.[14] The "sketch" to which Browere refers may be the *View of Stockton*

FIG. 67. A. D. O. Browere, *Jamestown or D. O. Mills' Mill,* ca. 1855. Oil on canvas mounted on Masonite board, 28⅛ × 38 in. California Historical Society, San Francisco, purchase.

now in the collection of the Oakland Museum of California (fig. 69), which is very similar to *Stockton,* his most ambitious version, created in 1856 (fig. 68).[15]

Browere is credited with skillfully portraying a community that burgeoned from a tiny settlement (originally called Tuleburg after the reeds that proliferated in the nearby marshlands) to a bustling trade center. All three views show Stockton once it had become established, with its original canvas structures replaced by more permanent buildings, first of wood, and then—when those proved vulnerable to the rampant fires that continually plagued this area—of brick. There is a brickyard in evidence on the far side of the river.

Although Browere depicts specific structures and a viewpoint "looking east toward the head of the Stockton Channel and the center of town," he managed to project "an idyllic, picturesque vision of the young city, focusing on those other resources—breathtaking expanses of sky, abundance of fish and wildlife, and a colorful, stable townscape—that might await the visitor hoping to find gold."[16] By its sheer scale, the 1856 painting emphasizes the bright clear sky, with snowcapped Sierra peaks in the distance. Although two fishermen row a boat in the middle ground, and a figure on the shore (which appears only in this version) hauls in a large net, the smooth surface of the water and egret in flight at the right endow the composition with a feeling of calm. With so few boats in the picture—there are two more boats at the left, one half-submerged in water, the other with sails lowered—there is little indication of the activity that the port surely sustained.[17]

In 1856, Browere returned to Catskill. He may have painted his large *View of Stockton* there, and certainly completed *Mokelumne Hill,* 1857 (fig. 70), while in the East. This composition, too, may have been developed from either pencil sketches or small paintings Browere made while in California. The fact that it was not painted from life may account for the lack of incident in the composition, other than the appearance of the red-shirted miner accompanying a mule cart in the foreground. Unlike most of Browere's other California landscape paintings, which feature waterfalls and fantastic rock forms, *Mokelumne Hill* shows a serene view across a valley into the Sierra. The ruts in the road and sparse trees indicate the impact of mining activities (including extensive logging to construct housing) on this area, but Browere nonetheless offers a beautiful scene. This painting is reminiscent of the Hudson River school compositions in its organization and details, but offers a more expansive view. Such an approach—certainly stimulated in part by the broad vistas that surrounded him—has been identified as the chief feature distinguishing Browere's California landscape paintings from his earlier views. And, as with his paintings of Stockton, the quiet view here gives little indication of Mokelumne Hill's distinction in boasting a fifty-mile canal that brought water to the mine sites or of its thriving population

FIG. 68. A. D. O. Browere, *Stockton,* 1856. Oil on canvas, 36⅞ × 69⅞ in. Fine Arts Museums of San Francisco, Museum Purchase. 39.3

FIG. 69. A. D. O. Browere, *View of Stockton,* 1854. Oil on canvas, 16 × 28 in. Oakland Museum of California, Kahn Collection.

FIG. 70. A. D. O. Browere, *Mokelumne Hill,* 1857. Oil on canvas, 34½ × 40½ in. The Bancroft Library, University of California, Berkeley.

during the early 1850s, when it was home to nearly eight thousand French miners alone.[18]

Two years later, in 1858, Browere set out again for California, this time traveling by way of Panama. Because he had spent considerable time in mining towns on his earlier trip, he was surely aware of the uncertainties that confronted gold-seekers, particularly late arrivals. His second trip may have been motivated by a desire to make further studies for Gold Rush paintings, or to relive the drama of the historic events in which he had participated.

Although they are undated, Browere may have painted his two scenes of the Chagres route, *The Trail of the '49ers* and *Crossing the Isthmus* (figs. 71 and 73), shortly after he reestablished himself in California. Both paintings show the verdant tropical foliage that inspired awe even in passengers exhausted after their arduous journey from the East.[19] In each painting, Browere places the imposing mountain at the center, a device he commonly employed, perhaps to lead the viewer's eye into space.[20] These symmetrical compositions appear idealized, and offer romanticized interpretations of the challenging thirty-eight-mile passage across the Isthmus, which could take early travelers a week or more to negotiate.[21] *Crossing the Isthmus* particularly shows a romanticized view, as the mules carrying the group of would-be miners had been superseded by the Panama Railroad by the time the artist made this trek. Close compositional parallels between *Crossing the Isthmus* and Thomas Cole's 1840 painting, *The Voyage of Life: Youth* (fig. 72), indicate that Browere was still looking to prototypes by other artists to compose his paintings. In choosing Cole's model, he apparently intended to give his landscape symbolic meaning rather than present a realistic view of a scene he encountered. This approach found favor with local patrons; *Crossing the Isthmus* was purchased by a collector in California.[22] Most likely Browere's *Goldminers* of 1858 (fig. 74) was also painted after his return to California. Again, the scene it

FIG. 71. A. D. O. Browere, *The Trail of the '49ers,* 1852 or 1858. Oil on canvas, 33 × 48 in. The Newark Museum, N.J., Edward F. Weston bequest.

FIG. 72. Thomas Cole, *The Voyage of Life: Youth,* 1840. Oil on canvas, 52½ × 78½ in. Munson-Williams-Proctor Institute Museum of Art, Utica, N.Y.

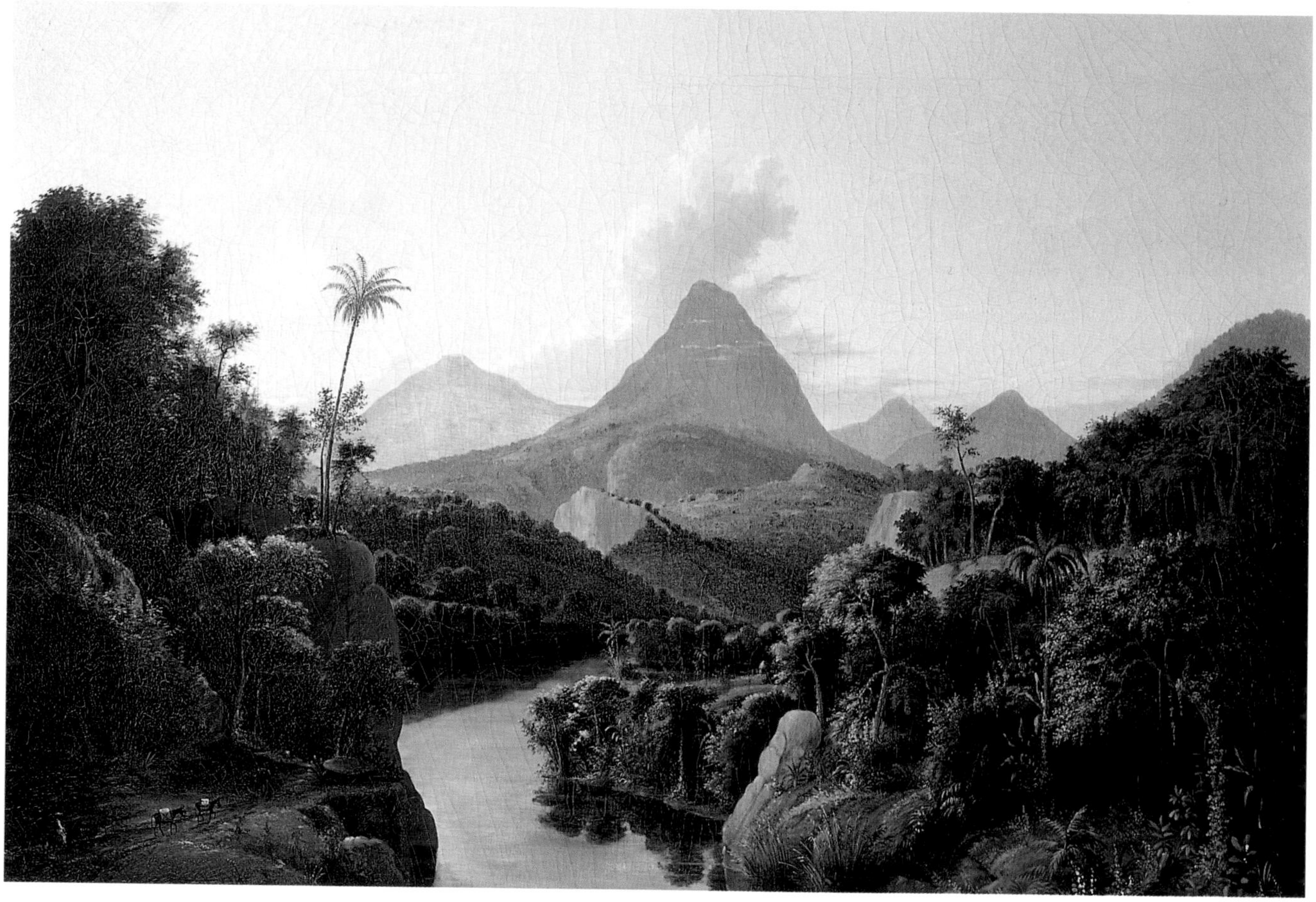

FIG. 73. A. D. O. Browere, *Crossing the Isthmus,* ca. 1858. Oil on canvas, 33 × 48 in. Crocker Art Museum, Sacramento, Calif., gift of the Crocker Art Museum Association.

depicts—a small group of miners taking a break from working a diverted stream—harks back to the beginning of the Gold Rush, suggesting that, as with *Crossing the Isthmus,* Browere was already painting retrospective views, capturing the flavor of the early years at the mine sites, where—as John David Borthwick and others noted—food was eaten in haste, and many miners gambled or consumed hard liquor when breaks allowed.[23] The six figures concentrated in the center foreground against a backdrop (here a washed-away hillside), repeat a compositional scheme for narrative subjects that Browere employed earlier.

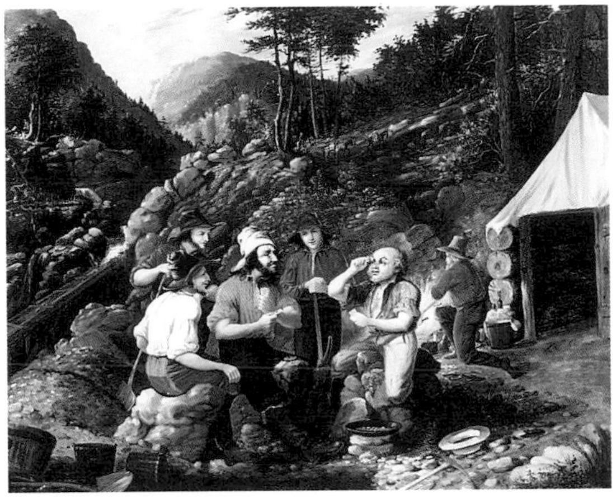

FIG. 74. A. D. O. Browere, *Goldminers,* 1858. Oil on canvas, 29 × 36 in. Anchutz Collection, Denver, Colo.

With *Goldminers* Browere uses figures that appear to be types rather than individuals. Picks, shovels, gold pans, and cookware give insights into the daily lives of the miners who are gathered here. The two cardplayers and the three miners who observe them form the center of attention, and are balanced by the rushing water at the left and the miner preparing food behind. Browere expended considerable care on the background landscape, where four mules—one bearing a red-shirted miner similar to *The Lone Prospector* he had painted several years earlier—are nearly hidden on the trail above the camp.

FIG. 75. A. D. O. Browere, *South of Tuolumne City,* 1861. Oil on canvas, 30 × 44 in. Oakland Museum of California, Kahn Collection.

Browere, who is listed as an "artist" in the 1859 San Francisco directory, completed a "large allegorical painting for a San Francisco Odd Fellows' celebration that year." By July 1860, however, he had returned to Columbia, and was mentioned in the *Tuolumne Courier* as "now doing portrait painting, landscapes, fancy and ornamental and decorative painting—Saloon and Housepainting when ordered."[24] It therefore appears that Browere again sought to support himself in the smaller mining communities, and—toward this end—returned to decorative painting. Despite the assessment that "this talented artist, so long identified with the history of Columbia, is now in Stockton, doing very well in his profession," there is little evidence that Browere achieved success with his painting in California.[25] Indeed, only a single painting, *South of Tuolumne City,* 1861 (fig. 75), was definitely produced during Browere's second stay in California, and there is little evidence of his activity during this time.[26]

In 1861, Browere left California permanently to return to Catskill. Little is known of his career after that, although he continued to work, painting signs and register boards as late as 1886.[27] He also apparently created some additional California scenes, and is noted as having exhibited such subjects after the Civil War.

Ironically, although Browere often relied on other sources for his compositional schemes and experienced difficulty in successfully integrating his figures and backgrounds, he was an innovator in painting Californian landscape vistas and mining life. He was one of the first to make large oil paintings of the surrounding scenery, and already by the mid-1850s was conscious of the importance of the early days of the Gold Rush and their rapid passing. In creating images of those events at a time when Americans had little interest in the Forty-niners as national figures and disparaged them as "down-at-the-heels Easterners hoping to strike it rich in California,"[28] Browere showed foresight. Remarkably, he produced a significant number of Gold Rush subjects, with apparently little support for his efforts. Both his charming landscapes and nostalgic genre scenes anticipate the flourishing of California landscape painting and romanticized depictions of Gold Rush subjects that occurred later, in the 1870s and 1880s.

In the Wake of the Gold Rush

FREDERICK A. BUTMAN, ALEXANDER EDOUART, AND GEORGE TIRRELL

Janice T. Driesbach

By the mid-1850s, artists were attracted to California not so much by gold as for other reasons. Mining was now less of an incentive to immigrate than were the state's stunning geography and excellent climate, not to mention its flourishing economy. With the advent of the Industrial Exhibitions of the Mechanics' Institute in 1857, which offered new opportunities to exhibit art, and San Francisco's establishment as a thriving metropolis, artists could expect the benefits of increasing patronage. Whatever their individual motivations, painters continued to flock to San Francisco in the late 1850s and early 1860s. Several of them, including Frederick Butman, Alexander Edouart, and George Tirrell, made compelling images of communities that drew directly from the events of the Gold Rush.

Frederick Butman, who arrived in 1857, has been credited as the first resident artist in California to devote himself exclusively to landscape painting.[1] His painting *Surveyor's Camp* (fig. 76), of the following year, is one of six views of the 1853 Pacific Coast Geodetic Survey that Captain W. E. Greenwell commissioned from Butman and other artists, including the Nahl brothers. That Butman was chosen to execute one of the scenes indicates that he had quickly established his reputation in San Francisco. Whereas the Nahl family had long been held in esteem as California artists, Butman's recent arrival postdated the event that he was asked to depict. His disposition of the seven tents at the camp and many of the details—including the dark and white horses paired at the right and the small white dog at the left center—are markedly similar to one by the Nahls.[2] However, the buildup of the distant hills in a sweep toward the upper right differs strikingly from the interpretation offered by the Nahls, calling into question the extent to which the various artists may have been working from a common source. The location is not identified in either painting.

Although most likely self-taught, Butman soon came to attention as an artist. Two paintings of Yosemite that he exhibited in the windows of Jones, Wooll & Sutherland, an art-supply and framing store, in late 1859, were described as "particularly worthy of notice for the rich coloring and the truthfulness to nature which the artist has observed throughout."[3] Significantly, Butman went to Yosemite at the same time that Jewett and other artists were making expeditions there, attracted by the splendid scenery and perhaps ready to exploit the new landscape subjects that California offered.

The following year Butman reportedly secured a local sponsor who underwrote the artist's

FIG. 76. Frederick Butman, *Surveyor's Camp,* 1858. Oil on canvas, 12½ × 18½ in. The Bancroft Library, University of California, Berkeley.

journeys to remote areas of California and Oregon. On this and subsequent trips, he gathered material for paintings of Lake Tahoe, Mount Shasta, Mount Hood, and other subjects. These continued to receive praise in the local press, and the artist was noted as "delight[ing] in large distances, high mountains, bright sunlight and brilliant coloring." By the 1860s, however, Butman's pictures were being criticized as "full of gaudy colors, and look as if they had been painted to sell; they have not the finish nor the fidelity to nature which alone gain the approval of judges."[4]

Although Butman's views of West Coast scenic landmarks were commented on in the press, two beautiful compositions of subjects close to home failed to attract attention. Perhaps painted as pendants, *Hunter's Point* (fig. 77) and *Chinese Fishing Village* (fig. 78) each offers views of established communities along the west side of San Francisco Bay. Despite its placid appearance, *Hunter's Point* shows a variety of activities occurring along the shoreline, from a young couple in conversation to Chinese fishermen on the beach. A well-dressed man, rifle in hand and peering back over his shoulder, sits astride a white horse. The white moldings and broken fence around the building that has fallen into disrepair immediately above him seem out of character with the unpainted wooden structures huddled toward the land's end, contributing to the mysterious quality of this image.

In contrast, *Chinese Fishing Village* is a more cohesive composition as well as an important historical document. The canvas represents one of the two earliest Chinese fishing settlements in California, at Rincon Point, near the footings of the present San Francisco–Oakland Bay Bridge. The village was established in the early 1850s, and by 1853 some 150 men in this community who operated 25 boats had pioneered California's saltwater fishing industry.[5] "Butman's scene substantiates research indicating that the Chinese fishermen 'lived in small fishing villages of their own construction somewhat removed from other parts of the population. . . . Their villages were located along the waterways . . . and consisted of large, unpainted redwood cabins built on stilts out over the beaches or directly over water.' The bustling composition also records the industriousness of the fishermen, who are shown engaged in a variety of activities, including work on sampans that are believed to have been constructed in California from Chinese models."[6]

Another engaging view of a distinctive community in California is Alexander Edouart's painting *Blessing of the Enrequita Mine* (fig. 79) of 1860. Arriving in San Francisco from the East Coast in the early 1850s, the British-born Edouart had traveled up the coast to Mendocino and the Noyo River area by 1857. He made a series of paintings of subjects he encountered there. He was represented in the *First Industrial Exhibition of the Mechanics' Institute* with what were listed only as "portraits in oil." The extended catalogue entry describes Edouart's depiction of an elderly man as "remarkably fine," and took

FIG. 77. Frederick Butman, *Hunter's Point,* ca. 1859. Oil on canvas, 24¼ × 36½ in. California Historical Society, San Francisco, gift of Albert M. Bender.

FIG. 78. Frederick Butman, *Chinese Fishing Village,* 1859. Oil on canvas, 23½ × 36 in. California Historical Society, San Francisco, gift of Albert M. Bender.

"occasion to congratulate the public that the artist now resides among us," but noted that, having been painted in Italy, the portrait failed to qualify for an award.[7] For some reason—perhaps because he hoped to encourage portrait commissions—Edouart must have chosen to enter a work that he had painted as a student nearly a decade earlier.

Edouart's finest California paintings are his two versions of the dedication of the quicksilver mines at New Almaden. In contrast to the watercolor *Mining in California* (see fig. 24), Edouart's composition shows a specific event, the dedication of the Enrequita Mine before it was opened in 1859. The view shows Mexican and Chilean miners and their families assembling for the blessing that will be given by Father Goetz, the Catholic curate of San Jose. The custom of offering blessing to the mine, those present, and its workers was well established. The festive nature of the event, which would be followed by fireworks, is indicated by the presence of the musicians in the background. Steam rising from the lower right makes reference to the furnaces located below. The assembled figures simultaneously tipping their hats toward the altar create a strong center of interest. Edouart also prominently featured three horses in the foreground, and frames the crowd with portraits of the Eldridge brothers, who owned the mine. Because one version of *Blessing of the Enrequita Mine* descended through the Eldridge family, it seems likely that they commissioned Edouart to document the event. The product is a striking portrayal of early California life, characterized by brilliant color and attention to detail in both costumes and landscape.

Although his ambitious composition reflects favorably on his skills, Edouart, for whatever reason—most likely either the time that painting entailed or lack of sufficient patronage—soon turned his attention to photography, establishing a successful practice first in San Francisco and later in Los Angeles.

Another painter who had only a brief career as an artist in California was George Tirrell. Little is known about him, but he was accomplished enough to have produced two distinguished achievements. A monumental *Panorama of California* (now lost) was first exhibited in San Francisco in April 1860 and met with considerable success. An exquisite painting titled *View of Sacramento, California, from Across the Sacramento River* (fig. 80), which has been dated to between 1855 and 1860, may have been executed in preparation for the panorama. A luminous composition, it offers some insights into how Tirrell represented California during its transition from the heady days of the Gold Rush to a time of increasing settlement accompanied by commercial and agricultural growth. In contrast to John Woodhouse Audubon's portrayal of the city some years before (see fig. 28), Tirrell's scene shows a busy harbor and a fair-sized city. Seen from the west, Sacramento's city hall and waterworks appear at the far left. With

FIG. 79. Alexander Edouart, *Blessing of the Enrequita Mine,* 1860. Oil on canvas, 29½ × 47½ in. The Bancroft Library, University of California, Berkeley.

more than fifteen boats of many types represented, the view gives evidence of the artist's love of sailing. Most prominently represented is the *Antelope,* a sidewheel steamship that was constructed in the East but had transported passengers between San Francisco and Panama during the heyday of the Gold Rush.[8] The paddleboat, barge, rowboats, and other craft all indicate continuing activity along the Sacramento River in the years following.

Tirrell, Butman, and Edouart were thus responsible for recording the effect of the Gold Rush on the subsequent development of industries and urban centers in California. Not only did the discovery of gold stimulate growth, but also—as their paintings testify—the arrival of would-be miners from throughout the world meant that people of many cultures participated in and contributed to the communities and commerce that developed in its wake.

The community of artists in San Francisco was likewise becoming established by the late 1850s. With the *First Industrial Exhibition of the Mechanics' Institute* in 1857, portraits by the San Franciscans Charles Christian Nahl and Edouart, among others, were featured alongside landscapes by John Henry Dunnel, wood engravings and watercolors by Harrison Eastman, and drawings by August Wenderoth. In all, nearly fifty artists were represented, some by single pieces, others by six or more. Not only was this display of work extremely popular—"continually crowded with admiring spectators" reported the *Daily Alta California*—but also it won considerable acclaim in the local press.[9] The report of the exhibition—published the following year—noted that "the judges . . . express their surprise and gratification at the rapid strides which the fine arts have made in our infant city, and their pleasure at the appreciative spirit of its citizens, without whose encouragement no elegant art would flourish. . . . There can no longer be a doubt that the State possesses an abundance of artistic talent, yearning to evolve itself, and fertile as our soil."[10]

The exposition was repeated a year later and again well received. Works by Thomas Ayres (who, by the time the fair opened on 2 September 1858, had perished in a shipwreck), Frederick Butman, the brothers Hubert and George Henry Burgess, and numerous others met with great acclaim. Reflecting the public's interest in the arts, the *Daily Alta California* devoted three columns to its review of the fine arts section.[11] In the ensuing years, the Mechanics' Institute exhibitions continued, at first irregularly (after the 1858 show, the next one was held in 1860) and then annually from 1874 until 1891.

In the meantime, talented artists such as Samuel Marsden Brookes (California's preeminent nineteenth-century Californian still-life painter), the marine specialist Gideon Jacques Denny, and the landscape painter Thomas Hill, had settled in San Francisco, and Albert Bierstadt made the first of two visits there. In 1864, the fine arts were accorded a separate display space at the Mechanics' Exhibition and a

FIG. 80. George Tirrell, *View of Sacramento, California, from Across the Sacramento River,* ca. 1855–60. Oil on canvas, 27 × 48 in. Gift of Maxim Karolik for the M. & M. Karolik Collection of American Paintings, 1815–65, courtesy Museum of Fine Arts, Boston.

second major public display of artwork (organized by William Smith Jewett and accompanied by an auction to which artists contributed) was offered with the Ladies' Christian Commission Fair in the fall. These events laid the groundwork for the founding of a local art union in early 1865, when "there were about thirty professional artists in the city." Like art unions in other American cities, the organization was founded for "the cultivation of the fine arts and the elevation of popular taste," and it sponsored an art gallery. Its initial reception was enthusiastic—"at the end of three months the membership numbered five hundred and the visitors were more numerous than ever before"—but the organization soon foundered.[12] However, momentum for increasing support for the arts was in place. The opening of the Snow and Roos Gallery in 1867 and the founding of the San Francisco Art Association in 1871 provided new exhibition spaces for artists, and when the Art Association opened its California School of Design in February 1874, Northern California boasted galleries and teaching facilities commensurate with its status as a thriving arts community.

FIG. 81. Charles Christian Nahl, *Sunday Morning in the Mines,* 1872. Oil on canvas, 72 × 120 in. Crocker Art Museum, Sacramento, Calif., E. B. Crocker Collection.

Sentiment and Nostalgia

CHARLES CHRISTIAN NAHL, ERNEST NARJOT, GEORGE HENRY BURGESS, HENRY BACON, AND RUFUS WRIGHT

Harvey L. Jones

MUCH OF THE ART CREATED during that first decade following the historic discovery of gold at Sutter's Mill in 1848 has itself become historically important as the beginnings of the visual arts tradition in California. Because the gold that served as impetus for their quest remained elusive for most of the artists, they soon reverted to the profession for which they trained. Initially their work was largely documentary: The Argonaut artists chronicled the places and events surrounding this epic phenomenon in drawings and paintings that functioned as eyewitness accounts. Soon the most talented and best-trained artists established their studios in the cities of Sacramento and San Francisco, where they offered a variety of artistic services to a growing population of prosperous patrons.

The artists, whose numbers were relatively small in the early years of the Gold Rush, were joined by printmakers and the practitioners of the growing art of photography to establish a rapidly developing community of artists and patrons that was flourishing by the end of the next decade. San Francisco emerged as the principal art center. As early as 1854, the owners of a book and stationery store converted the second floor of their premises into an art gallery, and hotel lobbies provided exhibition spaces for local artists.[1] Other opportunities for public showing, such as the Mechanics' Institute and state fairs, established in the late 1850s, served the Gold Rush artists as well as the influx of new arrivals in the 1860s.

During the Gold Rush, artists were called upon to provide their services as designers and illustrators for commercial applications that included panoramas, product labels, posters, pictorial letter sheets, membership certificates, advertisements, and book illustrations. Prominent artists such as the Nahl brothers, Harrison Eastman, George Burgess, and others drew hundreds of pictures for lithographs and engravings that were distributed throughout the world. These were the defining images of the Forty-niners and the scenes of the Mother Lode that have become enduring icons of the California Gold Rush.

Although few of the artists who searched for gold in the Mother Lode found much of the precious ore, they did discover metaphoric gold in the spectacular California landscape. Most Gold Rush paintings were genre scenes of mining activities and depictions of the lives of the Forty-niners. The landscape was, however, ever-present, sometimes insistent. Argonauts such as Thomas Ayres, George Burgess, and Frederick Butman were among the first artists to depict the wondrous scenery of the Yosemite Valley and the Sierra Nevada in the late 1850s, scenery that attracted a host of landscape painters from the eastern seaboard and Europe during the next two decades. The landscape tradition began to dominate California painting in the 1860s with the visits of such painters as Thomas Hill, William Keith, Albert Bierstadt, Virgil Williams, Julian Rix, and Juan Buckingham Wandesford, whose paintings of the wilderness became the new icons of California.

The artists' own efforts toward a cooperative organization, unsuccessful at first, eventually culminated in the founding of the San Francisco Art Association in 1871. A group of resident artists, art patrons, and interested citizens met at the home of Wandesford to create an appropriate venue for regular exhibitions and patronage. Several of the artists who had arrived in the Gold Rush and were still in San Francisco, including George Burgess, Ernest Narjot, and Charles and Arthur Nahl, became members or frequent exhibitors. In 1874 the association established the first art academy in the West, with Virgil Williams as its director. Known then as the California School of Design, it continues today as the San Francisco Art Institute.

By the 1870s the public perspective on the Gold Rush era had significantly changed. Once an appreciation of the vicissitudes of daily life in a rough and tumble frontier, it had become a feeling of nostalgia for the colorful events of the Gold Rush as recounted from the selective memories of surviving Argonauts or interpreted by writers of fiction. Charles Christian Nahl, who through paintings and lithographic illustrations had been responsible for creating so many of the images associated with life in the Gold Rush, returned to the theme in the 1870s.

Nahl's somewhat lugubrious subject of the *Dead Miner,* n.d. (fig. 82) was apparently derived from the last stanzas of an anonymous poem, *Winter in the Mines,* for which the artist provided seven vignettes to illustrate the text on a page published in the January 1859 issue of *Hutchings' Illustrated California Magazine.*[2]

WINTER IN THE MINES

Lost! lost, upon the mountain top—
So thickly falls the snow,
In vain he turns—the path is lost—
He knows not where to go.
His faithful dog still follows him—
The miner has one friend,
Who will attend him faithfully
Unto his journey's end.

And soon it comes, worn out, he falls
Upon the snow drifts high,
No friend to hear his mournful calls—
No one to see him die,
Except his dog, which constant still,
Leaves not his master's side,
But bones of both, in future, will
Mark where the wanderers died.

FIG. 82. Charles Christian Nahl, *Dead Miner,* n.d. Oil on canvas, 20 × 30 in. Autry Museum of Western Heritage, Los Angeles.

The inspiration for the image of a fallen miner lying in the snow beside his howling dog appears to have been an engraving for Matthieu Laurent's *History of Napoleon,* drawn by Nahl's mentor, Horace Vernet. In Vernet's illustration, a lone soldier lying dead is guarded by his dog.[3] It is not known when or for whom Nahl's sentimental version of the subject was painted. Records show that it was exhibited in the Mechanics' Institute Fair of 1876.

Both the *Dead Miner* and Nahl's most famous painting, *Sunday Morning in the Mines,* 1872 (fig. 81), had originated as lithographs during the late 1850s, and both took on subjective aspects of Gold Rush nostalgia, one sentimental, the other moralistic. In commissioning *Sunday Morning in the Mines,* Judge E. B. Crocker requested a painting typical of the life of the times. It remains the most important

FIG. 83. Charles Christian Nahl (attrib.), *Forest Burial,* n.d. Oil on canvas, 24 × 32 in. Collection of Eldon and Susan Grupp.

genre painting on a Gold Rush subject. Charles Nahl brought together all of his accumulated knowledge of painting and the imagery of the Gold Rush to create his masterpiece of narrative painting. For his story about miners of good and bad moral character, Nahl has given equal space to each issue in a composition that is divided in half vertically. The artist has distributed his principal dramatis personae along diagonal lines that begin at the lower corners of the painting and converge at a point above the center division to form a triangle that divides the rectangular format into multiple triangular shapes. The left side of the painting depicts the irresponsible activities of miners who are drinking, gambling, brawling, racing, and wasting their gold. The right side of the painting shows other miners engaged in more virtuous and industrious pursuits that include washing clothes, reading the Bible, and writing letters in their quiet observance of the Sabbath.

The artist's moralistic allegory extends to his representation of still-life elements depicted in the foreground of the painting. In the sunlit portion on the right side, we see the implements of productive living: the mining equipment, the cooking utensils, and the wood-chopper's ax. In the symbolic dark shadows of the shrubbery in the left foreground is scattered the discarded refuse of an ill-spent life that includes an empty whiskey bottle. The snowcapped peaks of the Sierra Nevada rise toward the sky in the distant background behind a Native American encampment that serves as a reminder of what was there before the arrival of gold-seekers. The iconography and all essential elements of the composition had been worked out by Nahl for an illustration titled *Sunday in the California Diggings,* dated 1857. He had already sketched themes for some of the vignettes as early as 1851.

Another painting on the subject of death in the Gold Rush era is a work that has recently been attributed to Charles Christian Nahl, *Forest Burial* (fig. 83). The unsigned sketch is apparently a preliminary study for a larger, unsigned painting of the identical subject that has been previously attributed to another artist. In a darkly wooded setting among yellow pines and sequoia trees somewhere in the Sierra, the artist depicts a group of four miners beside the open grave of a fallen comrade as they prepare to commit him to his final rest. Shown standing on a freshly dug mound of earth are three men with shovels poised as a fourth man stands beside the empty shroud, head bowed, hat in hand, in silent tribute before the grave of his departed friend. The artist has arranged the figures in a tightly structured pyramid shape within the overall landscape composition to impart a quality of ritual formality appropriate to the solemn occasion. The range of colors used in this study include the characteristic lavender, red violet, red orange, and russet hues of Charles Nahl's distinctive palette.

In the 1870s and 1880s, when the dramatic events of the California Gold Rush began to take on mythic dimensions in the memories of many Forty-niners, the genre painters joined the novelists, playwrights, poets, and songwriters of the day in their romantic re-creations of the days of gold. Ernest Narjot was among those artists whose artful representation of lives of the miners, remembered or imagined, survive as chronicles of California's history.

Narjot's painting, *The Forty-Niner,* 1881 (fig. 84), is indicative of the changes in pictorial representation of Gold Rush themes from a realistic to a nostalgic perspective. This spacious interior view of a miner's cabin contrasts sharply with the crowded confines shared by several men depicted in Charles and Arthur Nahl's *Saturday Night in the Mines,* from 1856 (see fig. 42). Narjot's painting presents a casual atmosphere of domestic self-sufficiency in a cozy one-man cabin outfitted with the traditional comforts of home. The French miners appeared to bring the comforts of civilized life with them. J. D. Borthwick, the artist—and occasional miner—who published an account of his three years in California during the early 1850s, specifically remarked on this propensity.

FIG. 84. Ernest Narjot, *The Forty-Niner,* 1881. Oil on canvas, 40 × 50 in. Santa Barbara Museum of Art, Calif., gift of Marguerite V. West and Mr. Charles H. King.

FIG. 85. Ernest Narjot, *Miners: A Moment at Rest (Gold Rush Camp),* 1882. Oil on canvas, 40 × 55½ in. Autry Museum of Western Heritage, Los Angeles.

> Of all the men of different nations in the mines, the French were most decidedly those who, judging from their domestic life, appeared to be the most at home. Not that they were a bit better than others able to stand the hard work and exposure and privations, but about all their huts and cabins, however roughly constructed they might be, there was something in the minor details which bespoke more permanency than was suggested by the generality of the rude abodes of the miners. It is very certain that . . . they did "fix things up" with such a degree of taste, and with so much method about everything, as to give the idea that their life of toil was mitigated by more than a usual share of ease and comfort. [4]

Narjot's painting is not merely a pictorial documentation of observable facts, but also an artistic interpretation of a concept. The artist has taken pains to provide a wealth of specific details in various still-life groups of objects that allude to basic needs in the miner's daily life: the placer miner's tools of pick, pan, and shovel; the handy dipper in a bucket of drinking water; the tabletop eating utensils with tin cup and plate; laundry drying on a clothesline above a glowing fireplace; and the miner's bed, complete with a flour-sack pillow, all of which set the stage for a brief, sentimental episode as the Forty-niner, seated beside his faithful dog, reads a letter from home during a moment of relaxation. Narjot's idealized scene of the solitary miner's life away from the daily diggings is a poetic reflection on the virtues of hard work and the rewards of a simple life. The physical hardships of the miner's actual life, as described in 1852 in one Argonaut's letter, are little in evidence:

> A Person thinking of coming to California ought to consider whether he can stand to work all day, under a hot sun, up to the knees in water and mud, shoveling or pumping as the case may be; cook his breakfast, and his supper at night, chop wood, bake bread, wash and mend clothes, &c. If he is content to do all these things and run the risks of the journey, then he can come to California. If not, he is better at home.[5]

Ernest Narjot's nostalgic tableau *Miners: A Moment at Rest (Gold Rush Camp),* dated 1882 (fig. 85), is an artful re-creation of a day in the lives of a company of Forty-niners, and a reflection upon Nahl's *Sunday Morning in the Mines.* Narjot's depiction of a group of miners at leisure closely parallels the theme of the virtuous miners represented in the right half of Nahl's epic allegory of morality in the Gold Rush. The miners' leisure activities in *Miners: A Moment at Rest* include a game of cards that appears to be merely a pleasant pastime, not a means for gambling. Narjot's composition follows Nahl's example by first directing attention to the central group of figures and next leading the observer's eye from one still-life vignette to the next around the edges of the painting before bringing it to rest again on the tight arrangement of figures depicted at the doorway of the cabin. The artist has developed a chain of visual

FIG. 86. Ernest Narjot, *French Gold-Seekers in California,* 1884. Oil on canvas, 15½ × 23 in. Collection of James McClatchy.

contact between the figures that focuses attention on the bearded man reading the newspaper. The influences of Nahl's painting extend to the remarkable similarity in the appearance of the bearded central characters in both pictures. However, Narjot's painting technique, executed in the loose, spontaneous brushwork of the mid-nineteenth-century French manner, is representative of a sophisticated "modern" approach popular in the 1880s that owes very little to the crisp definition and polished surfaces of Nahl's distinctive, but by then passé, style.

Ernest Narjot was only one among the great influx of French citizens from all levels of society that arrived in San Francisco in the early years of the Gold Rush. People of many professions and occupations came to make their fortunes and to add their contributions to California's cultural blend.[6] Narjot celebrates his own pride as a pioneer of French origin in his nostalgic 1884 depiction *French Gold-Seekers in California* (fig. 86). It is conceivable that the artist included himself among the three prospectors panning for gold in this iconographic Gold Rush genre painting. The narrative aspect of the scene is conveyed by expressions of anticipation revealed in the faces of the men whose attention is focused on the gold pan. Consequently, Narjot has also directed the viewer's attention to the depicted pan—perhaps to see a few of the precious nuggets.

By the late 1870s San Francisco was already a culturally well-established city with a growing arts patronage. Some of the city's elite citizens wished to celebrate San Francisco's progress with paintings that would document its Gold Rush origins. As part of this nostalgia, James C. Flood commissioned George Burgess to paint a fixed memory of the city, *View of San Francisco in 1850* (fig. 87).

Since his arrival in 1850, George Burgess had been an eyewitness to much of the early development of San Francisco. In 1878, when Burgess undertook the commission, he augmented his own memory of the city with references to other visual documents created on the spot in 1850. For his *View of San Francisco in 1850,* Burgess enlarged the image from a sketch made by John Prendergast, another English-born artist, many of whose historically accurate city views and depicted events were translated into lithographs and book illustrations.[7]

Burgess produced his own preliminary watercolor study of this historic San Francisco scene for the Silver King, James C. Flood, as well as another related watercolor with the same title for Sam Brannan. It was Brannan,[8] himself a prominent figure in the city's history, who established San Francisco's first newspaper, *The California Star,* and was widely reputed to have been the man who first brought news of the gold discovery to San Francisco.

The panoramic *View of San Francisco in 1850* looks east from the Clay Street hill on which are a number of tents pitched by prospectors in transit. The view extends toward the old Grand Plaza (Portsmouth Square), which originally was almost at the waterfront. Beyond the wharves at the center of the painting can be seen the many ships, abandoned by crews afflicted with gold fever, that block San Francisco harbor. In the background is Yerba Buena Island, the distant hills of Alameda and Contra Costa counties in the East Bay, and the present sites of Oakland and Berkeley. Burgess has re-created a moment in history with an unpretentious view of San Francisco that depicts virtually every building standing in the spring of 1850. Interesting genre touches include a cattle roundup at far left, the long queue at the post office on Clay Street near center right, and a couple of men on horseback pausing to chat with two women and a child at the right foreground.

Historical paintings of this type seemed to be part of a growing nostalgia for the Gold Rush that occurred some thirty years after the discovery of gold. Many of the Forty-niners had begun to reinterpret their memories of a great adventure in individual enterprise as something more selfless—part of a greater national achievement. Literature, popular song, poetry, and the visual arts were all part of a romantic reevaluation of this event. Nostalgia for the Gold Rush embraced the complete range of human experience with idealized and often sentimental depictions of the past as popular in literature as in painting. Bret Harte, San Francisco's first literary master, came to California in 1854 as a school-

FIG. 87. George Henry Burgess, *View of San Francisco in 1850,* 1878. Oil on canvas, 41 × 72 in. Private collection, courtesy of Hirschl & Adler Galleries, N.Y.

teacher before trying his luck as a miner. He became editor in 1868 of the *Overland Monthly* in San Francisco, a publication in which many of his own stories and poems were initially published. His descriptions of the lusty, humorous, and sometimes tragic life of mining camps in the Mother Lode are part of America's cultural legacy from the Gold Rush. Harte's earliest and best-known work is *The Luck of Roaring Camp,* a sentimental story of an orphaned infant adopted by a community of reckless miners and gamblers, whose lives were affected by the responsibility. Death was not uncommon in the mining settlements, but a birth was rare. This story inspired more than one artist to paint his version of the event. Henry Bacon, a talented artist from Boston who had trained at the Ecole des Beaux-Arts in Paris, painted *The Luck of Roaring Camp* in 1880 (fig. 89). He chose to illustrate the scene in which the anxious crowd of men arrived at the cabin to view the newborn citizen of Roaring Camp—whom they named Luck. The baby boy was wrapped in red flannel and placed in a wooden candle-box resting on a crude pine table and next to an upturned hat. "Gentlemen will please pass in at the front door, round the table, and out at the back door. Them as wishes to contribute anything toward the orphan will find a hat handy."[9] Virtually the same scene was chosen for an undated illustration titled *He Rastled with My Finger,* by Frederic Remington, and a similar painting, another *Luck of Roaring Camp,* from 1884 by Oscar Kunath (fig. 88).

FIG. 88. Oscar Kunath, *The Luck of Roaring Camp,* 1884. Oil on canvas, 42¼ × 55⅜ in. Fine Arts Museums of San Francisco, gift of Mrs. Annette Taussig in memory of her husband, Louis Taussig. 26562

FIG. 89. Henry Bacon, *The Luck of Roaring Camp,* 1880. Oil on canvas, 30 × 47½ in. Post Road Gallery, Larchmont, N.Y.

Harte's stories may also have been the inspiration for a Gold Rush subject by Rufus Wright, an American painter of anecdotal genre scenes. *The Card Players,* 1882 (fig. 90), is a depiction of the interior of a mountain cabin in which three men, a miner, a gambler, and a gun-toting cardplayer, cardsharps all, are playing euchre with a young Chinese man stereotypically depicted. This whimsical tale of a Chinese gambler who "wins the pot" from three disgruntled white men might almost be an illustration of Harte's satirical ballad, *Plain Language from Truthful James* (also known as *The Heathen Chinee*), which swept the country in the 1870s.

A pervasive xenophobia was responsible for much of the hostility among racial and ethnic groups during the Gold Rush. The English-speaking American's fear and distrust of foreign miners, who were competing for the best claims, resulted in animosities that were sometimes reflected in the art and literature of the times. Hostility toward the Chinese reached a peak in San Francisco during the 1880s. In the aftermath of the Gold Rush, and with the completion of the transcontinental railroad in 1869, the great influx of industrious Chinese immigrant laborers was perceived by the white population to be the cause of widespread unemployment and the economic depression of the 1880s, which was exacerbated by the collapse of the Nevada silver boom in 1878.

A decline in the sales and commissions for paintings brought about by the depression prompted many artists to leave San Francisco permanently during the 1880s. Local artists complained also of a shift in artistic taste among San Francisco's wealthy patrons toward a preference for European art. By this time the San Francisco Art Association's California School of Design was training the first generation of California-born artists. Typically they would continue their art studies in Europe, usually in Paris, for a few years before returning to establish their own distinctive artistic legacy that by then, as much as fifty years later, owed little to the influence of the California Gold Rush beyond a healthy respect for the pioneer spirit.

FIG. 90. Rufus Wright, *The Card Players,* 1882. Oil on canvas, 24¼ × 29½ in. Oakland Museum of California, Kahn Collection.

Biographies of the Artists

Katherine Church Holland

JOHN WOODHOUSE AUDUBON (1812–1862)

The younger son of the great ornithologist John James Audubon, John Woodhouse Audubon, born in 1812, was taught to draw at an early age and spent much of his childhood roaming the countryside, gathering specimens of birds and animals and drawing from nature. In 1836, the entire Audubon family traveled to Europe, stopping first in England and Scotland, where young John honed his artistic skills, painstakingly copying portraits by Thomas Lawrence, Henry Raeburn, and Anthony Van Dyck. After a Grand Tour of the Continent, Audubon returned to America in 1836 and settled in the Hudson River valley. His life was punctuated with forays as far as Texas and Europe, where he gathered specimens and painted from zoological collections, assisting in the preparation of his father's famous publications on the birds and mammals of North America.

In 1849 Audubon joined the California Company, a group of friends led by Colonel Henry L. Webb, destined for the West Coast and its golden bounty by a route via New Orleans and overland through the little-known terrain of Mexico. Audubon felt that this journey would give him a special opportunity to collect specimens of rare birds and animals. The journey was a tragic one. Besieged by robbers, abandoned by its leader, plagued by illness and death, the group struggled west. Despairing, many of the volunteers decided to return home, while the remainder voted to continue under Audubon's stewardship. Saddled with additional responsibility and confronted by ongoing challenges, Audubon used what precious time he had to sketch the countryside and record his impressions, hoping he could later create finished watercolors and oil paintings from them. Delayed by travails, the group was forced to cross the Mexican desert in the heat of summer. Eventually, after nine months, the remnants of the company reached San Diego in November 1849. Audubon left immediately for San Francisco and the gold diggings, sketching as he toured the mines.

In July 1850, Audubon departed for home, entrusting his collected sketches to friends for safekeeping and shipping. Unfortunately, the sketches were lost when the ship carrying them sank. Audubon's only surviving drawings were part of the journal he had sent to New York before his departure. From these, he published *Illustrated Notes of an Expedition through Mexico and California* in 1852, the first of what he had intended to be ten volumes on his experiences. The rest were never published. Audubon spent the remainder of his life in New York City, facilitating the publication of his father's work. He died there on 21 February 1862.

THOMAS A. AYRES (ca. 1816–1858)

A native of New Jersey, Thomas Ayres, born around 1816, moved with his family to Wisconsin as a young adult. Ayres showed an early interest in interpreting the landscape and, while employed as a draftsman in St. Paul, Minnesota, spent his leisure hours dabbling in oils and watercolors. Like numerous young men bent on adventure, he headed for California and guaranteed riches, boarding the ship *Panama* in New York on 4 February 1849, and arriving in San Francisco on 8 August. After disembarking in San Francisco, he headed directly for the mines, eager to find immediate wealth. But the promise of a swift fortune soon gave way to reality and the necessity to earn a livelihood. Switching from shovel to pencil and crayon, Ayres began sketching his surroundings, first around Tuttletown, and then, from 1850 to 1854, throughout the state, recording the burgeoning mining towns and the rugged landscape bordering the western edge of the continent.

Perhaps Thomas Ayres is best known as a member of the first tourist party to behold the wonders of Yosemite Valley. Rumors of the valley's beauty had long circulated, but until 1855 it had been explored only by Native Americans and military expeditions. In that year, James Mason Hutchings, planning a periodical, *Hutchings' Illustrated California Magazine,* proposed that Ayres record Yosemite, and in June Ayres accompanied a group led by Hutchings into the awe-inspiring canyon. First sketching at Inspiration Point, Ayres then drew twelve other views, among them a wide-ranging panorama and close-ups of El Capitan and Yosemite Falls. After revisiting the valley to make more drawings the following year, Ayres moved to New York City where his works were exhibited at the American Art Union. Commissioned by the Harper brothers to illustrate a series of articles on California for their publication, *Harper's Weekly,* Ayres returned to California, stopping in San Francisco in early 1858, and then setting out to sketch in southern California. After completing the southern segment of his journey, Ayres embarked for San Francisco on the schooner *Laura Bevan* in April 1858. The night of 26 April the ship foundered and sank off Point Dume, killing all aboard.

HENRY BACON (1839–1912)

The lure of gold in the raucous West was matched, for some, by the magnetic pull of the Ecole des Beaux-Arts in Paris. This prestigious school offered courses in classical painting, sculpture, and architecture that, especially from the early 1860s on, drew would-be artists not only from France and other European countries but also most particularly from America. One of the first fledgling American painters to turn to the Beaux-Arts for tutelage was Henry Bacon. Born in Haverhill, Massachusetts, in 1839, the son of a Universalist minister, Bacon had spent much of his youth in Philadelphia. Nothing is known of Bacon's early training in art, but he was, by the age of twenty-one, listed as an engraver in Boston's city directory. By 1861 he was designated as "artist" and had become a member of Boston's professional art community.

His early career was interrupted by the Civil War. Bacon volunteered and served until he was badly wounded at the Second Battle of Bull Run in 1862. After his discharge he painted with Winckworth Allan Gay, a landscape painter trained in Paris, but Bacon soon discovered that his own talents lay in figuration. Convinced that training in figure painting was limited in Boston, Bacon sailed for Paris in the spring of 1864 and enrolled at the Ecole des Beaux-Arts in the atelier of Alexandre Cabanel. Bacon remained in Paris for twenty-five years, studying, exhibiting regularly in the annual Parisian salons, and painting in a style that trod a narrow path merging tradition and fashion. Eschewing Impressionism as "crude," Bacon developed a mode of genre painting that appealed to Americans who, in the aftermath of the Civil War, were redefining their style and seeking new adventures in exotic places. His painting *The Luck of Roaring Camp,* for instance, evoked the boisterous days of the Gold Rush, though Bacon evidently never set foot in California. He also wrote two books, *A Parisian Year* (1882) and *Parisian Art and Artists* (1883). During the last years of his life, Bacon turned to watercolor, a portable medium that enabled him to paint during his many travels throughout Italy and the Middle East. Early in the 1900s he settled in London, where he spent his summers, and traveled each winter to Egypt where he painted extensively. He died in Egypt in 1912.

ALBURTUS DEL ORIENT BROWERE (1814–1887)

Known as much for his scenes of the Hudson River as for those of the goldfields of California, A. D. O. Browere was born in Tarrytown, New York, on 17 March 1814. His father, John Henry Isaac Browere, a sculptor, had perfected a system of making life masks of eminent Americans, and it was he who introduced his son to the basics of art. Young Browere, more interested in painting than in sculpture, may have studied briefly at the National Academy of Design in New York, where he began exhibiting in 1831. He soon developed a reputation as a portrait and history painter, exhibiting at the American Academy of Fine

Arts, New York, in 1833, the Apollo Association, New York, in 1838 and 1839, and the American Art Union, New York, in 1848. Although the artist moved in 1834 to Catskill—a site made famous by the artists of the Hudson River school—Browere listed his address as "Brooklyn" in 1844, indicating that he maintained close connections with New York City until at least the mid-1840s. To earn a living, Browere worked as a drugstore clerk and as a carriage and sign painter, activities that limited the time he could devote to painting. Perhaps influenced by his surroundings and the milieu of the Hudson River, he gradually turned from figurative and history painting to landscapes.

Enticed by the stories emanating from the West about the discovery of gold, Browere sailed around Cape Horn in 1852 and, probably after working as a carriage painter for a short time in San Francisco, headed for the mining regions. Settling in Columbia in mid-1854, he took up painting local landscapes, genre scenes portraying life in the mines, and portraits of pioneers. In 1856 Browere returned to Catskill carrying numerous paintings and sketches that he later worked up into finished pieces. Two years later he again journeyed west, taking the arduous route along the Chagres River through Panama, an experience he recorded in drawings and paintings. He settled in San Francisco, where he immersed himself in the cultural life of the burgeoning city but took many trips into the gold country. It may be conjectured that the motivation for this second trip to California was a desire to make further studies for works based on his experiences during the halcyon years of the search for gold. In 1861, Browere returned home to Catskill where he concentrated on his painting, reliving on canvas the early days of the Gold Rush. He died, in Catskill, in 1887.

GEORGE HENRY BURGESS (1830–1905)

One of four brothers to come to California from England in search of the good life, George Henry Burgess was born in London on 8 June 1830. As a young man he studied at the Somerset House School of Design in London and embarked on a comfortable career as a lithographer there. But the call of gold emanating from California proved irresistible. His eldest brother, Edward, had ventured to San Francisco in 1847 and had established a lucrative trading business between California and Hawaii, then called the Sandwich Islands. Another brother, William Hubert —called Hubert—immigrated to New York and California in 1850, and it was he who urged his younger siblings George and Charles to head west. The two set off for San Francisco that same year, taking the overland route after a transatlantic crossing. Like so many Argonauts, the Burgesses hastened directly to the Mother Lode where, following a short, marginally successful attempt at prospecting, they opened a jewelry business in Sonora, in the southern reaches of the mining region.

Political unrest between Americans and foreigners in the area forced the brothers to abandon their business, and George moved to San Francisco, working for a time as a lithographer with Britton and Rey, one of the earliest and most successful art and commercial lithography companies in the city. In 1853, the brothers left for the Sandwich Islands, where George sketched, painted, and printed, concentrating on views of Honolulu and picturesque scenes of the native peoples. Returning to the mainland, George joined Hubert in the jewelry trade, selling finely crafted pieces made from gold excavated from the mines. In 1858 George, again thirsting for gold, ventured into the wilderness of the Fraser River just north of what is now the Canadian border. Shortly thereafter he returned to San Francisco, established a studio specializing in portraiture, and began taking his place in the local art community.

His oeuvre soon expanded to include miniatures,

genre scenes, and landscapes, often inspired by his many hunting trips. Like the other prominent San Francisco artists of the day, his works were included frequently in the exhibitions presented by the Mechanics' Institute starting in 1857, and in 1871 he became a founding member of the San Francisco Art Association. His work was included in the association's exhibitions beginning in 1872 and culminated in the showing of his masterwork, *San Francisco in July, 1849* (fig. 60), at the Mark Hopkins Institute of Art in September 1900. George Henry Burgess lived in San Francisco and Berkeley until his death, in Berkeley, in 1905.

FREDERICK A. BUTMAN (1820–1871)

A native of Gardiner, Maine, where he was born in 1820, Frederick Butman received no formal art education and in fact owned an apothecary shop in his hometown from 1849 to 1857. During this period he began drawing and painting, producing figure studies and landscapes that were much admired by members of his community. After his arrival in San Francisco in 1857, Butman began recording and interpreting the vistas of his new homeland. His work was included in the expositions organized by the Mechanics' Institute in 1858 and 1864, and in the California Art Union exhibition in 1865; he was awarded a first prize at the California State Agricultural Society Fair of 1859. Butman's search for new views to paint took him to Yosemite and the Sierra Nevada beginning in the late 1850s and to the mountainous regions of Washington Territory in the early 1860s.

After a sale of his paintings at H. M. Newhall & Co., San Francisco, in 1866, he returned east in 1867, settling in New York. There, he exhibited at the Fifth Avenue Art Gallery and the National Academy of Design, and, in Philadelphia, at the Pennsylvania Academy of Fine Arts. Following a short sketching tour of Europe, Butman again set up residence in San Francisco in 1869 and resumed his career as a landscapist. After another sale of his work, which included views not only of the West Coast but also of New England and Europe, Butman left for the East in the spring of 1871 and died there unexpectedly on 26 July 1871.

JOHN HENRY DUNNEL (1813–1904)

For John Henry Dunnel (sometimes spelled Dunnell) art was but a pastime in a life filled with business and politics. Born in Millbury, Massachusetts, in 1813, Dunnel probably moved to New York City as a young man. There he earned his livelihood in commerce but spent his leisure time painting views of the New York and New Jersey countryside, which he exhibited at the National Academy of Design in 1847 and 1848.

Dunnel soon joined the avalanche of gold-seekers heading for the West Coast. He journeyed the treacherous route through Panama, then boarded the Pacific Mail steamer, the *Oregon,* and headed north, arriving in San Francisco on 1 April 1849. Dunnel didn't linger in the clamorous port, heading immediately for the Mother Lode. He established a business in Coloma and, when California was elevated to statehood, was elected by the community as its first Justice of the Peace. His interest in art continued, although the only known works by Dunnel during this period are three views of Sutter's Mill, just outside Coloma. Dunnel returned to New York early in 1851. He took an active role in Republican party politics, and was closely allied with his friend John C. Frémont, whose presidential bid in 1856 Dunnel supported enthusiastically.

Dunnel returned to California in 1857 as representative for the Singer Manufacturing Company and spent the following three years working from his office in San Francisco. But his painting activities continued and he exhibited two canvases—one a view of the Catskills—in the *First Industrial Exhibition of the Mechanics' Institute* in 1857. By 1860 Dunnel was back in New York City, where he remained until his death on 25 January 1904.

HARRISON EASTMAN (1823–1886)

A native of New Hampshire, where he was born in 1823, Harrison Eastman arrived in California on board the *Rodolph,* as part of the Shawmut and California Company bound for the goldfields. The brig had left Boston in February and reached San Francisco's port in September of 1849. Although there is no record of his having received formal art instruction before embarking for the West, Eastman soon found work as a wood engraver, lithographer, and, for a short period of time, as a clerk in the San Francisco post office.

A couple of months after the company arrived, the members reboarded the *Rodolph* and sailed to Sacramento, where they sold the ship in November. Eastman resumed work as a lithographer and wood engraver in Sacramento, taking on such projects as designing the seal of the city and creating the masthead for the local newspaper, the *Sacramento Transcript.* By mid-1850, Eastman had returned to San Francisco where he was sought after for his engravings, lithographs, paintings, and drawings of the Bay Area. Works such as *The Miner's Ten Commandments,* engraved on wood by Anthony and Baker after Eastman's designs, and *Lombard, North Point and Greenwich Docks, San Francisco,* drawn on stone by Eastman and Arthur Nahl after sketches by C. B. Gifford, secured Harrison Eastman's reputation. Several of his wood engravings and watercolors were included in the *First Industrial Exhibition of the Mechanics' Institute* in 1857. His *Scene in Montgomery Street in 1851* was awarded a diploma for best watercolor in the exhibition.

From 1857 to 1861, Eastman produced illustrations for James Hutchings's periodical, *Hutchings' Illustrated California Magazine.* In 1859 he and his partner, Pascal Loomis, founded the firm of Eastman and Loomis in San Francisco, specializing in engraving. The business lasted until Loomis's death in 1878. Eastman died in 1886.

ALEXANDER EDOUART (1818–1892)

The son of a prominent British silhouette artist, Alexander Edouart was born in London on 5 November 1818. After receiving instruction in Edinburgh, Scotland, Edouart traveled to Italy where he studied art in 1847 and 1848. In 1848 Edouart immigrated to New York City, where he remained until 1852, exhibiting at both the National Academy of Design in 1849 and 1850 and the American Art Union. Traveling by the clipper ship *Queen of the East,* Edouart arrived in San Francisco on 8 September 1852. It is presumed that he spent at least some of the ensuing five years in the mining regions, but by 1857 he had settled in San Francisco and established a studio on Montgomery Street.

His paintings were included in the *First Industrial Exhibition of the Mechanics' Institute* held in San Francisco in 1857 and, that same year, he accompanied a hunting party to the Mendocino area, where he sketched his fellow travelers and the headquarters of the Mendocino Indian community. The following year he returned to that area, painting the military post at Fort Bragg and sketching a view of Round Valley. In 1859 Edouart visited England and France and, shortly after his return to San Francisco, he turned his attention to photography, which he continued throughout his life. In 1889 Edouart moved to Los Angeles, where he set up a photography studio with his son, Alexander Edouart Jr. He died on 6 November 1892 in Los Angeles.

AUGUSTO FERRAN (1813–1879)

Among the thousands who thronged to the goldfields were men of diverse nationalities and backgrounds. With the first wave of immigrants to San Francisco was Augusto Ferran, who arrived in early 1849. A native of Spain, where he was born in 1813 in Palma on the island of Mallorca, Ferran had gained a reputation there as a sculptor. After his initial art instruction at the

Accademia de San Fernando in Madrid, Ferran traveled to Paris to complete his formal education. The surviving works from this period indicate that he concentrated on classical and religious subjects as well as portraiture.

Accompanying Ferran to California was José Baturone, and together they recorded the men, fresh from the mines, who were eager to spend their newfound wealth. These humorous figure studies were issued as *Album Californiano* (also known as *Tipos Californianos*), a portfolio of twelve hand-colored lithographs published in Havana, Cuba, in 1849 or 1850 by Luis Marquier. While in California, Ferran also painted views of the San Francisco Bay Area, reflecting the extraordinary growth of the fledgling community in the early days of the Gold Rush. After leaving California, Ferran settled in Cuba where he taught at an art school in Havana. He died in Havana in 1879.

WASHINGTON F. FRIEND (ca. 1820–ca. 1886)

Born in Washington, D.C., around 1820 to English parents, Washington Friend was an accomplished musician, painter, and entrepreneur who founded a music academy in Boston in 1846 only to lose it to a fire the following year. He then established a short-lived "floating museum" on the Wabash River.

Beginning in 1849, Friend embarked on a three-year tour of Canada and the United States that took him not only through the provinces of Quebec and Ontario, but also to the eastern seaboard and western regions of the country: Colorado, Montana, Utah, and California. Throughout this tour, Friend sketched the places he visited, intending to expand and embellish his sketches into a finished opus. In New York City he realized his dream, painting a vast panorama that he then exhibited in major cities throughout the United States and Canada, as well as in London. Tremendously popular, the presentations took the form of entertainment: Each of the monumental scenes was accompanied by commentary and appropriate songs sung by Friend, and his preparatory sketches were displayed and available for purchase. These expositions continued at least into the 1860s. Queen Victoria herself viewed the spectacle and purchased some sketches in London in 1864.

Little is known about Friend's later years, although works by him depicting New England and the Hudson River in the 1880s are extant. He died around 1886.

E. GODCHAUX (dates unknown)

The Gold Rush was a magnet for French natives who flocked to California in search of a better life. By 1851 more than four thousand French citizens had migrated to the West Coast; two years later the number was estimated at thirty-two thousand. Many of these immigrants settled in the mining region—where they were often met with animosity—but others were attracted to the cities, becoming restaurateurs, journalists, wine merchants, and importers. Although nothing definite is known about this artist, he may have been part of the family of Adolph Godchaux who left Alsace in 1840 and lived in New Orleans for eleven years before traveling to San Francisco via Panama in 1851. Adolph established Godchaux Brothers and Company, an import and export business that thrived in San Francisco. It is also possible that the artist was the Edward Godchaux who exhibited an oil painting in the *Eighth Industrial Exhibition of the Mechanics' Institute* in 1871.

WILLIAM SMITH JEWETT (1812–1873)

On 17 December 1849, at the height of the influx of Argonauts into San Francisco Bay, William Smith Jewett arrived on the sailing ship *Hope,* eager to secure his fortune in the land of opportunity. Born in South Dover, New York, on 6 August 1812, Jewett had studied at the National Academy of Design in New York, and in 1845 had been elected an associate of the academy. Although he exhibited regularly and had established a seemingly successful career as a portraitist and landscape painter in New York, Jewett's initial aspirations in California lay not in art, but in the Hope Company, an association of New Yorkers determined to succeed in the mines. Following the dissolution of the company, however, Jewett turned his energies again toward the easel, rendering portraits of prominent merchants and politicians who wished to establish their positions in the new community or to reassure loved ones back home.

Jewett's reputation as a portraitist grew rapidly. Early in 1850 he established a studio in San Francisco, but in May of that year, after the studio was burned down in one of the fires that periodically ravaged the fledgling city, Jewett traveled to Coloma in the gold mining area, staying with the merchant John T. Little. During this visit, he painted a view of Sutter's Mill and the Coloma Valley—later translated into a lithograph by Sarony and Major—and tried his hand at panning for gold. Jewett also met with Andrew Jackson Grayson—a leading expert on the birds of western North America and himself an artist—and began work on *The Promised Land* (fig. 33), a landmark composition of Grayson and his family posed at the summit of the Sierra against a backdrop of the great Sacramento Valley.

In his studios in Sacramento—from 1850 to 1855—and in San Francisco—from 1850 to 1869—Jewett continued to render in oil the visages of the wealthy and the powerful. In 1855 he was commissioned by the California State Legislature to paint a full-length portrait of John A. Sutter. Two years later, the inclusion of *The Promised Land* in the *First Industrial Exhibition of the Mechanics' Institute* elicited a great public response. But, despite his popularity, Jewett lived a simple life and the income he earned through his art was carefully invested, particularly in real estate. By 1860, a concern for financial security and a growing feeling of homesickness pervaded his letters. He looked upon his painting primarily as a means of returning to his family. Nevertheless, his preparations to depart were time and again delayed by various financial ventures, as well as commissions he continued to accept. Eventually, in September 1869, Jewett left California and returned to New York, but his popularity there as a painter had subsided. After marrying Elizabeth Dunbar, the niece of Erwin Davis, one of his most important San Francisco patrons, Jewett visited the West Coast briefly in 1871, then embarked on a tour of Europe. This journey was cut short by illness and the Jewetts came back to the United States where the artist died on 3 December 1873 in Springfield, Massachusetts.

WILLIAM McILVAINE (1813–1867)

Born into a wealthy Philadelphia family on 5 June 1813, William McIlvaine attended the University of Pennsylvania where he received degrees in 1832 and 1835. During an extended tour to Europe following his graduation, McIlvaine inhaled the rich cultural ambiance of the continent, visiting museums and studying painting. Returning to the realities of Philadelphia, McIlvaine joined his father in the family business but maintained his interest in art, painting whenever time allowed. His landscapes of Europe were exhibited at the Artists' Fund Society of Philadelphia in 1840; by 1845 he had made the decision to become a professional artist, concentrating on landscapes.

In 1849 McIlvaine left behind the solid world of Philadelphia for the rough-and-tumble milieu of California. Arriving in San Francisco on 1 June 1849, he hastened to the mines, where he spent the summer drawing and painting the world of the gold diggings—the vivid character of the toilers, the emotional chaos of the communities. Returning to San Francisco in October, McIlvaine quickly headed for home on the steamer *California,* his sketches and paintings safely packed in his luggage. The following year McIlvaine published *Sketches of Scenery and Notes of Personal Adventure in California and Mexico,* a series of sixteen lithographs based on the drawings created during his visit west.

McIlvaine resumed exhibiting in Philadelphia during the 1850s, particularly at the Pennsylvania Academy of the Fine Arts, and in New York at the National Academy of Design. He moved to New York City in 1857 and served with the New York Zouaves during the Civil War, leaving the service in 1863. His last years were spent in Brooklyn where he died on 16 June 1867.

WILLIAM BIRCH McMURTRIE (1816–1872)

In response to the catastrophes that befell many of the ships heading for the calm waters of San Francisco Bay during the Gold Rush, the United States government initiated a coastal survey to map the Pacific coast and adjacent inland waters. Aboard the vessels that carried out this survey were artists, among them William Birch McMurtrie, who carefully recorded, with the eyes of artists and surveyors, the scenes they witnessed during these naval tours.

McMurtrie, born in Philadelphia in 1816, was the son of Dr. Henry McMurtrie, a scientist whose social circle included prominent citizens of the community. McMurtrie's early education is undocumented, although it is surmised that he may have studied with the painter and engraver William Russell Birch, for whom he was named. He did paint canvases, however, that were included in the exhibitions of the Artists' Fund Society of Philadelphia, intermittently from 1837 through 1845, and at the American Art Union, New York, sometime in the mid-1840s.

While living in Washington, D.C., in 1848, McMurtrie gained a position with the United States Coast Survey, starting as a temporary journeyman in topography. In late 1848 he accepted a post as draftsman on board the survey schooner *Ewing,* bound for the Pacific coast. Leaving New York on 10 January 1849, the ship headed for Cape Horn and California carrying McMurtrie, who sketched Rio de Janeiro and the coast of Argentina along the way. Arriving in San Francisco in September 1849, McMurtrie soon made several watercolors of the unruly community. The following spring the ship turned north, sailing up the California and Oregon coasts, and spent the summer surveying the Pacific Northwest. McMurtrie made numerous drawings during this tour, despite suffering acutely from rheumatism. McMurtrie continued his surveying studies of the coast and San Francisco Bay, punctuated by at least one visit back to the East Coast. His work was included in exhibitions at the Pennsylvania Academy of the Fine Arts, Philadelphia, in 1851, 1852, 1856, and 1857. Little is known of these years, although he may have spent part of the time in Colorado.

By 1859 he was back in Washington, D.C., focusing on the eastern and southern coasts with the Coast Survey. The ensuing years found him living and working in Washington, but exhibiting in Philadelphia until 1870. He died in Washington on 30 December 1872.

FRANCIS SAMUEL MARRYAT (1826–1855)

A talented adventurer whose gifts included not only artistic skills but also an aptitude for writing and acting, Francis Samuel Marryat came to California on a quest. Unlike many of his fellow seekers, his initial search was not for gold, but for the exotic game that abounded in the woods of California. Marryat embarked for California, not with pick and shovel, but with a manservant and three hunting dogs. The son of the novelist Captain Frederick Marryat, whose tales of naval derring-do were extremely popular in Victorian England, Francis—called Frank—was born in London on 18 April 1826. His earliest training was in seamanship: He joined the British navy when he was fourteen and remained in service for eight years. His naval career took him on far-flung voyages including tours of the Mediterranean Sea and the Indian Ocean.

Although no evidence points to formal art training, Marryat was brought up in a home environment filled with culture and drama. He embarked on his naval voyages armed with notebooks and sketchpads and, in fact, upon leaving the military, wrote his first book, *Borneo and the Indian Archipelago,* which was published in 1848 and illustrated by some sixty of his own woodcuts and lithographs. Eager for new adventures, Marryat boarded a ship for Panama, crossed the Isthmus, and headed for San Francisco, arriving on 14 June 1850 just as a great fire, which had leveled most of the city, was subsiding. For the next two years, Marryat led a peripatetic life, venturing north to the Sonoma and Russian River valleys to hunt deer and wildfowl, up to the northern diggings above Sacramento, and to the southern Mother Lode—Sonora and Tuttletown—where he tried his hand at quartz mining.

Family concerns pulled Marryat back to England in the spring of 1852, but he returned one year later, hoping to show the marvels of the West to his new bride. Sadly, although they had survived an outbreak of yellow fever on board the ship to California, they were greatly weakened and soon left for England and home. There Marryat completed *Mountains and Molehills, or Recollections of a Burnt Journal,* an account of his Gold Rush exploits in narrative and illustrations. The book, containing twenty-six engravings after his drawings, was published in 1855 and proved to be immensely popular. But Marryat was not destined to enjoy his newfound fame; he died of a ruptured blood vessel on 12 August 1855.

E. HALL MARTIN (1818–1851)

A native of Cincinnati, Ohio, E. Hall Martin, named Ezekial by his parents, was born into a poor family in 1818. Apparently self-taught and something of a prodigy, he was, it has been said, already painting professionally in Cincinnati by 1831 and, in 1846, was listed in that city's directory as a portrait painter. In 1847, he relocated to New York City. The following two years were spent executing portraits, genre scenes, and marine views, which he exhibited at the American Art Union in both 1847 and 1848. Heeding the call to adventure and riches in California, Martin booked passage in steerage aboard the *Panama,* which left New York in mid-February 1849, bound for Cape Horn and California. Included among the 220 souls on board was another artist, Thomas Ayres. Arriving in San Francisco on 8 August, Martin began painting, and, according to contemporary accounts, enjoyed some measure of popularity. But he was dogged with health problems including depression, and his endeavors with brush and pencil were frequently interrupted by periods of illness.

The summer of 1850 found Martin moving to Sacramento where he set up a studio. Eking out a meager living through various odd jobs and the occasional sale of his paintings, he continued to be plagued with poor health and at one time suffered from cholera. Over the next year, Martin periodically ventured from his Sacramento home base into the diggings, recording the miners and scenes of mining life. His existence remained precarious, however. In the fall of 1851, against the advice of his friends, Martin decided to go to the mountains to make some sketches for paintings that he could sell. During that trip, in December 1851, Martin died in Onion Valley, near Downieville, at the age of thirty-three.

CHARLES CHRISTIAN NAHL (1818–1878)

The pursuit of a career in the arts came naturally to Charles Christian Nahl, born in 1818 to an extended family that counted artists in their midst back to the seventeenth century. A native of Kassel, Germany, Nahl probably received his earliest training from his father, Georg Valentin Friedrich Nahl, a local etcher and engraver, and further instruction from his cousin Wilhelm, well known for his portraits and historical scenes. Nahl showed early promise as a watercolorist, and he augmented his early education by attending the academy in Kassel—where he took classes with Professor Justin Heinrich Zusch—and studying masterworks by Frans Hals, Rembrandt van Rijn, and Peter Paul Rubens, among others, in the local museum.

Nahl's career as a painter blossomed, but he soon felt the need for a more sympathetic cultural milieu and, motivated by the turmoil in his family's personal life, moved to Paris in 1846.

Nahl continued his studies in Paris, working with Horace Vernet and Paul Delaroche, copying Rubens in the Louvre and studying anatomy at the local medical school. He met with some success, exhibiting at the Salon in 1847 and 1848. But the political scene in the French capital, coupled with personal and financial problems, proved untenable and in 1849 Nahl, his family, and their friend, August Wenderoth, sailed for New York, settling in Brooklyn. Nahl's stay in the New York area proved brief but notable, for he exhibited at the American Art Union in 1849 and 1850 and sold enough works to finance a voyage to California in search of gold. Leaving New York in March 1851, Nahl, again accompanied by his family and Wenderoth, traveled via Panama and the Chagres River, arriving in San Francisco on 23 May.

The party hastened to the mines but, discouraged by their initial failures, soon took up pencil and paper, sketching the faces of the miners and their surroundings. By the end of 1851, they had left the foothills for the metropolis of Sacramento, where Nahl and Wenderoth opened a studio. The disastrous fire of 1852 prompted them to return to San Francisco. There they and Charles's half-brother, Arthur, established a business concentrating on lithographs, portraiture, and genre scenes. Nahl took an active role in the cultural life of San Francisco, frequently exhibiting his portraits, historical paintings, and scenes recounting the story of the Gold Rush at the Mechanics' Institute, starting in 1857, and the San Francisco Art Association and California State Fair. He and Arthur also promoted the community's enthusiasm for physical exercise. Their back yard became a favorite gathering place for friends who liked to pass their leisure hours at gymnastics and bodybuilding. These activities provided the genesis for the founding of San Francisco's Olympic Club, the first athletic club in America.

During the last years of his life, Nahl created his most renowned works, major paintings commissioned or purchased by such local dignitaries as Judge E. B. Crocker of Sacramento and Leland Stanford. He died of typhoid fever in San Francisco on 1 March 1878.

HUGO WILHELM ARTHUR NAHL (1833–1889)

The half-brother of Charles Christian Nahl, Hugo Wilhelm Arthur Nahl, known as Arthur, was born in Kassel, Germany, in 1833. He accompanied his family to Paris in 1846 at the age of thirteen and there was given his first instruction in art by Charles, who guided him through exercises in perspective and the then-mandatory drawing from plaster casts of classical sculpture. Formal studies followed at the local academy and in the galleries of the Louvre, Versailles, and Luxembourg Palace. The work of the young artist met with success; by the age of sixteen, he was awarded a gold medal by the academy for his accomplishments.

Political unrest in Paris prompted the Nahl family, accompanied by August Wenderoth, to sail for New York in 1849. Settling in Brooklyn, they exhibited at the American Art Union where Arthur, like his brother and friend Wenderoth, exhibited and sold works. Gold fever was then at its peak and the family, lured by the prospect of sure riches, sailed for California by way of Panama in early 1851. After arriving in San Francisco on 23 May, the group left immediately for the goldfields and tried their hands at mining, but with no success. After a year in Sacramento where Arthur worked as a woodcarver, the Nahls relocated in San Francisco and young Nahl collaborated with his brother and Wenderoth, often acting as assistant in the commissions secured by their studio. Shortly after his marriage to Annie Sweeney in 1865, Arthur and his bride settled in Alameda on the eastern shores of San Francisco Bay. He continued his work as partner in Nahl Brothers, eventually producing most of the commercial illustrations and portraits for the firm. His genre scenes, landscapes, portraits, and animal studies were frequently included in the exhibitions presented by the San Francisco Art Association and the California State Fair, and at other venues. Arthur Nahl died on 1 April 1889.

ERNEST NARJOT (1826–1898)

Among the many French natives who rushed to the goldfields in search of riches was Ernest Narjot, born in Brittany near St. Malo on 25 December 1826. The son of artists, Narjot shared his parents' enthusiasm for painting, and received a classical training in drawing and painting in Paris. Narjot set off for the New World in 1849, traveling around Cape Horn and arriving in San Francisco late in the year. Although he expected to establish himself as a professional artist in the thriving metropolis, Narjot found few patrons for his work. Disappointed, he quit the city for the mines, where he tried his hand at digging. Narjot did not, however, forsake his initial vocation. He continued to draw and paint, augmenting his income by rendering portraits of his fellow miners complete with the trappings of their lives. Narjot's lack of success in the diggings and failure to establish his art as a profession in San Francisco prompted him to seek his fortune elsewhere.

In 1852, Narjot joined a group of young French nationals on an expedition to the mines of Sonora, Mexico. The venture failed, but Narjot remained in Mexico and became moderately successful as a miner and an artist. He acquired and worked a silver mine while continuing to paint portraits, genre scenes, and landscapes of the local countryside and of southern California and Arizona. Following the overthrow of Emperor Maximilian, all French property in Mexico—including Narjot's—was confiscated, so in 1865 he returned to San Francisco, set up a studio, and embarked on an active career as a painter. His work was shown frequently: The Mechanics' Institute, the San Francisco Art Association, and the California State Agricultural Association included him regularly in their exhibitions. Well-known for his contemporary portraits and picturesque genre scenes, Narjot often also dipped into his past for subject matter, reprising scenes of the Gold Rush and life along the Mexican border. He executed major mural commissions in churches, theaters, and other public buildings. These activities culminated in the request by Mrs. Leland Stanford to decorate the tomb of her late husband. While painting the ceiling of the mausoleum, Narjot inadvertently splashed paint in his eyes, an incident that eventually led to total blindness. Narjot's last years were spent in destitution and he died 24 August 1898.

SAMUEL STILLMAN OSGOOD (1808–ca. 1885)

Portraiture, particularly of the wealthy and powerful, was a successful vocation for Samuel Stillman Osgood, who established one of the earliest portrait studios in San Francisco. Osgood, born in New England on 9 June 1808, was reared in Boston, where he first studied painting. By the age of twenty-two, he had executed a portrait of the frontiersman David Crockett. Three years later, in 1833, he married the poet Frances Sargent Locke, and together they traveled to Europe, where Osgood absorbed the rich cultural milieu and continued his pursuit of an education in art. His early efforts were in the field of genre painting, which he exhibited at the British Institute, London, in 1838 and 1839. He then returned to the United States, where he made New York City his home base although he was for short periods of time in Boston, Philadelphia, and Charleston, South Carolina.

Leaving a lucrative career in New York, Osgood embarked for California in 1849 and at first tried mining. Discouraged by his lack of success, he determined to try his luck as a professional artist in San Francisco. As he made his way from the Sierra foothills to the coast, he stopped at Sutter's Fort where he sketched a likeness of John Sutter. After establishing his studio in San Francisco, Osgood worked up his sketch of Sutter in oils, finishing it in September 1849. Two months later he carried it back to New York and the engraver John Sartain translated it into a print that, because of Sutter's fame, proved to be very popular. Returning to San Francisco and an admiring public in 1852 after another tour of Europe, Osgood launched into a profitable vocation capturing on canvas the faces and figures of prominent San Franciscans. In December 1853 Osgood again left San Francisco, not to return except for a brief visit made on his way to Japan in 1870. The last years of his life are shrouded in mystery. It has been thought that he spent an extended period living in California, but reports are sketchy. Samuel Stillman Osgood died around 1885.

JOHN PRENDERGAST (dates unknown)

Little is known of the life of John Prendergast, a British-born artist who arrived in San Francisco from Honolulu in 1848. It is presumed that Prendergast remained in California for at least three years as works signed by him and dated from 1849 through 1851 are extant, but no evidence points to his remaining past 1851. Prendergast concentrated on views of the burgeoning metropolis of San Francisco, but also recorded events of import to the community: the procession held to celebrate the admission of California to statehood in October of 1850, and the aftermath of the fire of 4 May 1851, for instance. He did venture outside the city—a drawing of Benicia and Martinez, located northeast of San Francisco on Suisun Bay, has survived. The date and place of Prendergast's birth and of his death are unknown.

W. TABER (dates unknown)

The early years of the Gold Rush found several individuals with the surname Taber arriving on the shores of San Francisco Bay. In August 1849 Isaiah West Taber disembarked from the *Friendship* out of Fairhaven, Massachusetts. The following month saw the arrival of his brother, Charles Austin Mendell Taber, and a William H. Taber, possibly another brother, who sailed on the brig *Rodolph* with Harrison Eastman. Their father, Freeman Taber, was a shipwright from Buzzard's Bay in Massachusetts where whaling and the sea were the dominant way of life.

Evidence points to all three having gone to the mines. C. A. M. Taber was by the end of September sending a considerable amount of gold dust back to his father and he appears to have captained a ferry boat between Sacramento and San Francisco. William probably sailed to Sacramento on the *Rodolph* with Eastman and a fellow passenger, George Kent. It is known that, by 1851, he was back in San Francisco where he was a member of the Vigilance Committee. Isaiah West Taber tried ranching and dentistry but by the 1860s he had become a photographer in San Francisco, establishing his own studio in 1871. It is possible that the creator of the drawing in this book (fig. 16) was either William H. Taber—about whom we know nothing after 1851—or Isaiah West Taber. Another suggestion for authorship is Isaac Walton Taber, who was a popular illustrator for books and magazines such as *Harper's Weekly, St. Nicholas,* and *Century Magazine* in the late nineteenth and early twentieth centuries. The drawing in the exhibition was published in *Century Magazine* in August 1891.

GEORGE TIRRELL (dates unknown)

Although the monumental *Panorama of California* was a sensation in its day, little is known about its creator, George Tirrell. There is a possibility that Tirrell arrived in San Francisco on the bark *Edward Fletcher,* on 5 March 1849, from Boston. He must have traveled throughout northern California sketching landmarks, for a painting by him of Sacramento, possibly datable to between 1855 and 1860, and a letter sheet are extant. We also know that he was employed by Robinson's Theatre, San Francisco, in 1860 as a painter of scenery.

For three years, starting around 1857, Tirrell

worked on his magnum opus, the *Panorama of California* (or *Tirrell & Company's Panorama),* a gigantic canvas reportedly measuring 11 by 175 feet. Depicting scenes from the northern Golden State, the sweeping painting was composed of four sections: the region from Benicia to Monterey, including scenes of historic events; the area from Sacramento north to Mount Shasta, including Marysville; the mining communities from Sierra Buttes, at the northernmost reaches of the diggings, to the Big Trees of Calaveras County; and the southern mining country from Columbia to the Yosemite Valley. This extravaganza on canvas, unveiled to its audience over a period of two and one-half hours, opened to acclaim at Tucker's Academy of Music on Montgomery Street in San Francisco on 25 April 1860. It subsequently toured to Marysville in June 1860 and perhaps traveled to other venues.

In 1861, at least three illustrations after drawings by Tirrell were published in San Francisco in *Scenes of Wonder and Curiosity in San Francisco.* Tirrell was active in New Orleans as a painter of scenes at the Varieties Theater in 1874–75. The dates of his birth and death are unknown.

FREDERICK AUGUST WENDEROTH (1819–1884)

Destined to become an artist, Frederick August Wenderoth, called August, was born the son of a painter, Carl Wenderoth, in Kassel, Germany, in 1819. His initial education in art came from his father, who taught him the rudiments of drawing; he continued his studies at the academy in Kassel and, by the age of around eighteen, young Wenderoth was giving lessons in the fundamentals of art to the ladies of the court at Hesse-Kassel, where his mother was a lady-in-waiting. Wenderoth quit Germany for Paris in 1845, but soon left again for Algiers before resettling in the French capital where he was joined by his friend and former colleague at the Kassel academy, Charles Christian Nahl, and his family. There, despite an unsettled political situation, the young artists visited the many art museums, particularly the Louvre, studying the work of the masters. In May 1849, the Nahl family, accompanied by Wenderoth, left Paris for New York, arriving at the end of June and settling in Brooklyn.

August Wenderoth's stay in New York was a successful one for he exhibited at the American Art Union where he sold nine paintings in 1849 and 1850. But by 1851 he had succumbed to gold fever and, again with the Nahl family, left New York for California via Panama. He arrived in San Francisco on 23 May, stopped only briefly, and then hurried to the Sierra foothills and the promise of riches. The anticipated fortune eluded Wenderoth and he returned to his original vocation, sketching the miners and, perhaps, making daguerreotypes of them. The end of 1851 found Wenderoth and Charles Christian Nahl in Sacramento, where they established themselves as specialists in portraiture, lithography, and wood engraving. After the disastrous fire of November 1852 in Sacramento destroyed their business, Wenderoth and the Nahls removed themselves to San Francisco and began again to thrive in the fields of lithography, illustration, wood engraving, and portraiture.

A voyage to the South Seas and Australia in 1852–53 was followed by Wenderoth's marriage in 1856 to Laura Nahl, the half-sister of Charles Christian. The young couple soon left for Philadelphia where, despite the death of his wife and newborn child the following year, Wenderoth established himself as a successful daguerreotypist, painter, and illustrator for *Harper's Weekly.* He died in Philadelphia of tuberculosis in 1884.

RUFUS WRIGHT (b. 1832)

Well known in his day for anecdotal genre scenes and portraits of distinguished political, judicial, and commercial figures, Rufus Wright was born in Cleveland, Ohio, in 1832. He received his art instruction in New York City at the National Academy of Design and from George Augustus Baker Jr., a painter of portraits and miniatures. Evidence points to a trip overland to the West Coast in the late 1850s—a drawing of Davenport, Iowa, executed in 1857 or 1858 by Wright, was made into a lithograph published by Sarony, Major, and Knapp in 1874—and it is known that he documented a Mormon community (most probably in Utah) in 1859. But by the end of 1859, Wright was back in New York. After a brief period spent in Washington, D.C., Wright moved to Brooklyn in 1864, and he remained there until at least 1886.

In Brooklyn, Rufus Wright was active in the art community. He was a founder of both the Brooklyn Art Social—in 1859—and the Brooklyn Academy of Design—in 1866—and a teacher at the academy for several years. He exhibited regularly at the National Academy of Design in New York from 1862 to 1880, and at the Brooklyn Art Association from 1865 to 1880. Among his portraits were those of such stellar contemporary figures as Roger Brooke Taney, the chief justice of the United States Supreme Court and an author of the *Dred Scott* decision, Edwin M. Stanton, Abraham Lincoln's secretary of war during the Civil War, and William H. Seward, the secretary of state under both Lincoln and Andrew Johnson. Wright's landscapes captured views in the Hudson River valley, the Adirondacks, New Jersey, and Pennsylvania; his genre scenes carried such titles as *"Thank You, Sir," Come Back Birdie,* and *The Inventor and the Banker.* It is not known where or when Wright died.

BIOGRAPHICAL SOURCES

Ackerman, Carl E. "In the Days of Forty-Nine." *Camera Craft* 2 (December 1900): 106–13.

———. "Across the Isthmus in Early Days." *Camera Craft* 2 (January 1901): 37–41.

Anderson, Nancy K. "Thomas A. Ayres and His Early Views of San Francisco: Five Newly Discovered Drawings." *The American Art Journal* 19 (1987): 19–28.

Arkelian, Marjorie. "An Exciting Art Department 'Find'." *Art* (Art Guild of the Oakland Museum Association) 2 (January–February 1974): n.p.

Audubon, John Woodhouse. *Audubon's Western Journal, 1849–1850.* Cleveland, Ohio: Arthur H. Clark, 1906. Reprinted with introduction by Frank Heywood Hodder and memoir by Maria R. Audubon. Tucson: University of Arizona Press, 1984.

Caughey, John Walton, ed. "Life in California in 1849: As Described in the 'Journal' of George F. Kent." *California Historical Society Quarterly* 20 (March 1941): 26–46.

Conkling, Roscoe. "Reminiscences of the Life of Albertus del Orient Browere." *Los Angeles County Museum of Art Quarterly* 8 (spring 1950): 2–6.

Dentzel, Carl Schaefer. Introduction to *The Drawings of John Woodhouse Audubon: Illustrating His Adventures through Mexico and California, 1848–1850.* San Francisco: Book Club of California, 1957.

Dressler, Albert. *California's Pioneer Artist Ernest Narjot: A Brief Resume of the Career of a Versatile Genius.* San Francisco: privately printed, 1936.

Evans, Elliot, ed. "Some Letters of William S. Jewett, California Artist." *California Historical Society Quarterly* 23 (June and September 1944): 149–77; 227–46.

———. "William S. and William D. Jewett." *California Historical Society Quarterly* 33 (December 1954): 309–20.

———. "The Promised Land." *Quarterly of the Society of California Pioneers* 36 (November 1957): 1–11.

Giffen, Helen S. "Blessing of the Enrequita Mine, New Almaden: Painting by Alexander Edouart, 1859." In *Treasures of California Collections.* San Francisco: Book Club of California, 1956.

Jewett, William Smith. Letters, 1849–71. The Bancroft Library, University of California, Berkeley.

Junkin, Sara Caldwell. "The Europeanization of Henry Bacon (1839–1912), American Expatriate Painter." Ph.D. diss., Boston University, 1986.

Kurutz, Gary F. "'California Is Quite a Different Place Now': The Gold Rush Letters and Sketches of William Hubert Burgess." *California Historical Society Quarterly* 56 (fall 1977): 210–29.

McIlvaine, William. *Sketches of Scenery and Notes of Personal Adventure in California and Mexico.* Philadelphia, 1850.

Marryat, Frank. *Mountains and Molehills, or Recollections of a Burnt Journal.* Introduction and notes by Marguerite Eyer Wilbur. Stanford, Calif.: Stanford University Press, 1952.

Monroe, Robert D. "William Birch McMurtrie: A Painter Partially Restored." *Oregon Historical Society Quarterly* 60 (September 1959): 352–75.

Reynolds, Gary. "The Landscapes of Alburtus Del Orient Browere." Paper, City University of New York Graduate Center, spring 1976.

———. "The Life and Work of Alburtus Del Orient Browere (1814–1887)." Master's thesis, Brooklyn College of the City University of New York, 1977.

Rogers, Fred B. "The Bear Flag Lieutenant, the Life of Henry L. Ford (1822–1860) Together with Some Reproductions of Related and Contemporary Paintings by Alexander Edouart." *California Historical Society Quarterly* 30 (June 1951): 168–71.

Stevens, Moreland L. *Charles Christian Nahl: Artist of the Gold Rush 1818–1878.* Exh. cat. Sacramento, Calif.: E. B. Crocker Art Gallery, 1976.

Vail, R. W. G. *Gold Fever: A Catalogue of the California Gold Rush Centennial Exhibition.* New York: The New-York Historical Society, 1949.

Van Nostrand, Jeanne. "Thomas A. Ayres: Artist-Argonaut of California." *California Historical Society Quarterly* 20 (September 1941): 275–79.

———. "Audubon's Ill-fated Western Journey Recalled by the Diary of J. H. Bachman." *California Historical Society Quarterly* 21 (December 1942): 289–310.

Wright, Charles G. "Albertus D. O. Browere 1814–1887: A Genre Painter of the Hudson River School and Resident of Catskill, N. Y., 1840–1887." Paper presented to the Greene County (New York) Historical Society, 1971.

Notes

INTRODUCTION: THE LURE OF GOLD

1. Walton Bean and James J. Rawls, *California: An Interpretive History* (New York: McGraw Hill, 1983), 85–87.

2. David Lavender, *California: A Bicentennial History* (New York: W. W. Norton and the American Association for State and Local History, 1976), 52–53; quoting Walter Colton, *Three Years in California* (New York: Barnes, 1850), 246–47.

3. Lavender, *California: A Bicentennial History,* 53.

4. Malcolm J. Rohrbough, *Days of Gold: The California Gold Rush and the American Nation* (Berkeley and Los Angeles: University of California Press, 1997), 25–27.

5. Owing to political turmoil and relatively sparse settlement, there are no exact figures on the size and composition of California's population in 1848.

6. Rohrbough, *Days of Gold,* 26.

7. David Lavender, *California: Land of New Beginnings* (Lincoln, Nebr.: University of Nebraska Press, 1987), 165–66.

8. Ibid.

9. Anthony Kirk, "In a Golden Land So Far: The Rise of Art in Early California," *California History* 71 (spring 1992): 2–23; an excellent overview of pre–Gold Rush art, including images created by members of exploration and survey parties.

10. Occupations are listed in ships' logs. See John E. Pomfret, ed., *California Gold Rush Voyages: Three Original Narratives* (San Marino, Calif.: Huntington Library, 1954), 95–96, 172–76.

11. "Journal of a Voyage from Boston, Mass. to San Francisco, California in the Brig *North Bend,* Capt. Higgins, by C. H. Ellis, Passenger," in Pomfret, ed., *California Gold Rush Voyages,* 12; see also Lavender, *California: A Bicentennial History,* 63, and Frank Marryat, *Mountains and Molehills, or Recollections of a Burnt Journal* (Stanford, Calif.: Stanford University Press, 1952), 156, 174, 304, 313, 381.

12. Jeanne Van Nostrand, *The First Hundred Years of Painting in California, 1775–1875* (San Francisco: John Howell-Books, 1980), 92; and Dudley T. Ross, *The Golden Gazette* (Fresno, Calif.: Valley, 1978), 29.

13. Benjamin Parke Avery, "Art Beginnings on the Pacific," *Overland Monthly* 1 (July 1868): 30.

14. *Report of the First Industrial Exhibition of the Mechanics' Institute of the City of San Francisco, September 7–26, 1857* (San Francisco, Calif.: Printed at the Franklin Office, 1858), 16.

15. John S. Hittell, "Art in San Francisco," *Pacific Monthly* 10 (July 1863): 99–107.

FIRST IN THE FIELD

1. Thomas A. Ayres, program accompanying the exhibition *California! On Canvas!* (collection, The Bancroft Library, University of California, Berkeley). See also Jeanne Van Nostrand, *The First Hundred Years of Painting in California, 1775–1875* (San Francisco: John Howell-Books, 1980), 42; Jeanne Van Nostrand and Edith M. Coulter, *California Pictorial: A History in Contemporary Pictures, 1786 to 1859* (Berkeley and Los Angeles: University of California Press, 1948), 136.

2. Van Nostrand, *The First Hundred Years,* 42, citing *Daily Alta California,* 7 August 1854.

3. Among drawings by Ayres that were reproduced as prints was an 1855 view of a pilot boat off the Golden Gate that was lithographed by Britton and Rey in San Francisco, as noted in John Haskell Kemble, *San Francisco Bay: A Pictorial Maritime History* (Cambridge, Md.: Cornell Maritime Press, 1957), 114. See also Nancy K. Anderson, "Thomas A. Ayres and His Early Views of San Francisco: Five Newly Discovered Drawings," *The American Art Journal* 19 (1987): 19–28.

4. Anderson, "Thomas A. Ayres," 22–24.

5. Ibid.

6. Van Nostrand, *The First Hundred Years,* 82.

7. *Sacramento Daily Union,* 1 June 1858, p. 4; Jeanne Van Nostrand, "Thomas A. Ayres: Artist-Argonaut of California," *California Historical Society Quarterly* 20 (September 1941): 275–79; Van Nostrand, *The First Hundred Years,* 82.

8. The artist's name is listed as Ezekiel Hall Martin in an article about him in the *Cincinnati Daily Mirror,* 1835.

9. Robinson & Jones's *Cincinnati Directory for 1846* ("first annual issue"): "Martin E. Hall, portrait painter, N E cor Vine and 5th [and Franklin]."

10. *Doggett's New York City Directory* (1847–48), 276: "E. Martin Hall, artist, 251 Broadway."

11. Mary Bartlett Cowdry, *American Academy of Fine Arts and American Art Union Exhibition Record, 1816–1852* (New York: The New-York Historical Society, 1953), 243. *Castle of San Juan Ulloa,* sold to Duncan Grant (New York) 1847, lot no. 36; *Boy Fishing,* sold to Edwin Croswell (Albany, New York), lot no. 376; *Marine View,* sold to George Campbell (Pittsfield, Mass.), 1848.

12. United States Department of the Navy, Office of the Chief of Naval Operations, Division of Naval History (OP 09B9), Ships' Histories Section: "History of Ships Named Somers," March 5, 1962, p. 1.

13. *Alta California,* 16 January 1850, p. 1, col. 3.

14. *The Illustrated California News* 1, no. 1 (1 September 1850), p. 7, col. 1. This periodical was published only from 1 September through 1 December 1850. No sketch of a "miner prospecting" (by Martin) was printed.

15. Inscription on reverse of painting: "Mr. A. Reynolds, Buffalo, Via China and Cape Good Hope, Favor of Capt. Johnson, Clipper Ship Invincible."

16. *Sacramento Transcript,* 20 December 1850, p. 2, col. 2.

SCENES OF MINING LIFE

1. Anthony Kirk, "In a Golden Land So Far: The Rise of Art in Early California," *California History* 71 (spring 1992): 8.

2. McIlvaine exhibited *Panning Gold,* under the title *Scene on the Tuolumne,* at the Pennsylvania Academy of the Fine Arts and the National Academy of Design during the 1850s. Jeanne Van Nostrand and Edith M. Coulter, *California Pictorial: A History in Contemporary Pictures, 1786 to 1859* (Berkeley and Los Angeles: University of California Press, 1948), 107.

3. *M. & M. Karolik Collection of American Water Colors and Drawings, 1800–1875,* vol. 1 (Boston: Museum of Fine Arts, 1962), 231.

4. Jeanne Van Nostrand, in *The First Hundred Years of Painting in California* (San Francisco: John Howell-Books, 1980), refers on page 56 to an early genre painting of the Gold Rush by McIlvaine as well as to several other landscapes by the artist.

5. Willard B. Farwell, "Cape Horn and Cooperative Mining in '49," *California Excerpts from Century Magazine* (August 1890–April 1902): 592.

6. Ibid.

7. When the swarm of immigrants to San Francisco resulted in an overwhelming increase in the amount of mail sent there, its postal officials were severely criticized. In an effort to improve service, Jacob B. Moore—who was from Eastman's hometown—was appointed San Francisco's postmaster. It is likely Eastman's employment was a result of his acquaintance with Moore. John Walton Caughey, ed., "Life in California in 1849: As Described in the 'Journal' of George F. Kent," *California Historical Society Quarterly* 20 (March 1941): 29–30.

8. Jeanne Van Nostrand, *San Francisco, 1806–1906 in Contemporary Paintings, Drawings and Watercolors* (San Francisco: Book Club of California, 1975), pl. 19.

9. In addition to his other activities, Eastman continued to produce original watercolors, including an early portrait of James Marshall (now at Marshall Gold Discovery State Park in Coloma) and a view of Sutter's Fort. He also received a prize for *A Scene in Montgomery Street in 1851* at the *First Industrial Exhibition of the Mechanics' Institute* in 1857. Eastman was an early teacher of William Keith, one of the outstanding late-nineteenth-century California landscape painters, and a contributor to the establishment of a community of artists in San Francisco. Van Nostrand, *The First Hundred Years,* 38; Brother Cornelius, *Keith: Old Master of California* (New York: Putnam, 1942), 17.

10. J. D. Borthwick, *3 Years in California,* with index and foreword by Joseph A. Sullivan (Oakland, Calif.: Biobooks, 1948), 132.

11. Malcolm J. Rohrbough, *Days of Gold: The California Gold Rush and the American Nation* (Berkeley and Los Angeles: University of California Press, 1997), 137.

12. James E. Henley, director, Sacramento Archives and Museum Collection Center, conversation with author, 30 May 1997.

13. Henry Winfred Splitter, "Quicksilver at New Almaden," *Pacific Historical Review* 26 (February 1957): 33–50.

14. Ibid., 41.

15. Ibid.; also citing James Butterworth Randol, "Quicksilver," in *Report on Mineral Industries in the United States at the Eleventh Census in 1890* (n.p., n.d.): 179–245.

16. John Woodhouse Audubon, *Audubon's Western Journal* (Cleveland: Clark, 1906), reprinted with introduction by Frank Heywood Hodder and memoir by Maria R. Audubon (Tucson: University of Arizona Press, 1984), 41.

17. John Woodhouse Audubon, *Illustrated Notes of an Expedition through Mexico and California* (New York, 1852), reprinted (Tarrytown, N.Y., 1915), 8.

18. Audubon, *Audubon's Western Journal,* 116–17.

19. Ibid., 189–95.

20. Ibid., 204.

21. Ibid., 223.

22. Ibid., 225–28.

PORTRAIT PAINTER TO THE ELITE

1. William Smith Jewett, 23 December 1849, in Elliot Evans, "Some Letters of William S. Jewett, California Artist," *California Historical Society Quarterly* 23 (June 1944): 155–59.

2. In the 1840s, Jewett exhibited at the National Academy of Design in New York, where he was made an associate. Reportedly, he received a commission to paint the governor of New York just before he left for California. However, while in the East, he does not appear to have achieved the "enviable reputation" attributed to him by Ferdinand C. Ewer; see Ewer, "The Fine Arts," *The Pioneer* 2 (August 1854): 112.

3. Jewett, 28 January 1850, in Evans, "Some Letters," 160.

4. Although Jewett regularly participated in exhibitions at the National Academy of Design while in New York, he was represented by only a single entry, his *Portrait of Washington A. Bartlett* in 1851, once he was in California. He did join the Society of California Pioneers in 1856 and contributed to the inaugural exhibition of the Mechanics' Institute the following year, but Jewett seems to have shied away from formal affiliations in San Francisco as well.

5. See note 3 above.

6. Ibid.

7. Ibid., 160–61.

8. Jewett, 30 January 1850, in Evans, "Some Letters," 162.

9. Ibid.

10. Ibid.

11. *Alta California* (San Francisco), 18 March 1850.

12. Ibid.

13. Elliot Evans, "The Promised Land," *Quarterly of the Society of California Pioneers* 36 (November 1957): 4.

14. Ibid., 4–5.

15. Dawn Glanz, *How the West Was Drawn* (Ann Arbor, Mich.: UMI Research Press, 1982): 61–62. Glanz notes that Jewett may have been familiar with Claude's painting from an engraving made of it during the eighteenth century, and discusses other biblical and Mosaic references in *The Promised Land,* including the allusion to the story of Moses and the Israelites in its title.

16. Evans, "Promised Land," 7.

17. Jeanne Van Nostrand, *The First Hundred Years of Painting in California, 1775–1875* (San Francisco: John Howell-Books, 1980), 46.

18. Of fifteen paintings Jewett exhibited in New York before he left, five were landscapes. Of these, two were views of the Hudson River from Poughkeepsie, one a view of Lakes Washuning and Washanee in Connecticut, and two were simply called *Landscape.* The American Art Union had purchased one of the latter two before its exhibition in 1847. See Mary Bartlett Cowdry, *National Academy of Design Exhibition Record, 1826–1860,* vol. 1 (New York: The New-York Historical Society, 1943), 267–68.

19. *Daily Alta California* (San Francisco), 11 February 1851.

20. Jeanne Van Nostrand and Edith Coulter, *California Pictorial: A History in Contemporary Pictures, 1786 to 1859* (Berkeley and Los Angeles: University of California Press, 1948), 117.

21. *Daily Alta California* (San Francisco), 5 April 1851.

22. Elliot Evans, letter (Archives of California Art, Oakland Museum of California, Oakland, Calif.).

23. Frank Marryat, *Mountains and Molehills, or Recollections of a Burnt Journal* (Stanford, Calif.: Stanford University Press, 1952), 347.

24. Ferdinand C. Ewer, "Editor's Table," *The Pioneer* 2 (August 1854): 112.

25. William Smith Jewett to the State Assembly, Sacramento, 27 April 1855 (Archives of California Art, Oakland Museum of California, Oakland, Calif.).

26. *Journal of the Sixth Session of the Assembly of the State of California* (Sacramento, 1855), 853, quoted in Evans, "Some Letters," *California Historical Society* 23 (September 1944): 245.

27. William Smith Jewett to the *Sacramento Daily Bee,* 21 October 1855, p. 3.

28. General John A. Sutter to the *Sacramento Daily Bee,* 21 October 1855.

29. Bernardine Swawley, research report (Archives of California Art, Oakland Museum of California, Oakland, Calif.).

30. *Daily Alta California* (San Francisco), 28 December 1856, p. 2.

31. William Smith Jewett, 7 January 1860, in Evans, "Some Letters," 227.

THE HESSIAN PARTY

1. Moreland L. Stevens, *Charles Christian Nahl, Artist of the Gold Rush, 1818–1878,* exh. cat. (Sacramento, Calif.: E. B. Crocker Art Gallery, 1976), 39.

2. Purchased, along with *Crossing the Plains,* by Jane Stanford from J. O. Coleman for $3,000, 27 September 1900.

3. Ada Kruse Ducker, "Charles Christion Nahl: Argonaut Artist" (The Bancroft Library, University of California, Berkeley), 28.

4. Stevens, *Nahl,* 133.

5. Lucius Beebe and Charles Clegg, *San Francisco's Golden Era* (Berkeley, Calif.: Howell-North, 1960), frontis.

6. Nahl family letters, 1842–76, portfolio (The Bancroft Library, University of California, Berkeley).

7. Ibid.

8. Arthur Nahl to Wilhelm Nahl, 2 April 1858, in Nahl family letters.

9. Stevens, 133.

10. Ibid., 81.

After Judge Crocker died, Mrs. Crocker, considering the paintings inappropriate for her museum, donated them to the Fine Arts Museums of San Francisco.

SOUVENIRS OF THE MOTHER LODE

1. Albert Dressler, *California's Pioneer Artist Ernest Narjot: A Brief Resume of the Career of a Versatile Genius* (San Francisco: privately printed, 1936).

2. J. D. Borthwick, *3 Years in California,* with index and foreword by Joseph A. Sullivan (Oakland, Calif.: Biobooks, 1948), 167.

3. Gary Kurutz, "'California is Quite a Different Place Now': The Gold Rush Letters and Sketches of William Hubert Burgess," *California Historical Quarterly* 56 (fall 1977): 211.

4. Ibid., 218.

5. George Burgess, to his mother (Archives of California Art, Oakland Museum of California, Oakland, Calif.).

6. Ibid.

7. Benjamin Parke Avery, "Art Beginnings on the Pacific," *Overland Monthly* 1 (July 1868): 34.

8. Joseph A. Baird Jr., "San Francisco in July of 1849" (archives of Hirschl & Adler Galleries, N.Y., n.d., photocopy), 5.

9. George H. Burgess, MS (Archives of California Art, Oakland Museum of California, Oakland, Calif., n.d.).

10. J. W. Willeirs, "San Francisco in July, 1849," research compiled for Warren E. Howell of John Howell Bookstore, San Francisco, 23 August 1977 (Archives of California Art, Oakland Museum of California, Oakland, Calif.).

11. Burgess MS.

12. See note 8 above.

MINING THE PICTURESQUE

1. Browere's first recorded contribution to a National Academy of Design exhibition was a painting titled *Midnight at Jericho* in 1831; two years later, his *Rip Van Winkle* was lent from the collection of a Mr. Wolf. He was represented by *Capture at Fort Casmir* in 1838, and with five paintings the following year, three subjects inspired by Washington Irving, *The Lone Indian,* and a "Sketch from Nature." After that time, Browere exhibited only four paintings at the academy, his last entry being *King Philip Relating His Wrongs to an Ally* in 1846. *National Academy of Design Exhibition Record, 1826–1860* (New York: The New-York Historical Society, 1943).

2. Mabel P. Smith and Janet R. MacFarlane, "Discovery and Rediscovery: Unpublished Paintings by Alburtis del Orient Browere," *Art in America* 46 (fall 1958): 68–71.

3. Gary A. Reynolds, "The Landscapes of Alburtus Del Orient Browere (1814–1887)" (City University of New York Graduate Center, spring 1976), 10–11. This paper and Gary Reynolds, "The Life and Work of Alburtus Del Orient Browere (1814–1887)" (master's thesis, Brooklyn College of the City University of New York, 1977), are the most substantial sources on the artist. I want to thank Dr. William H. Gerdts for sharing these materials and other information on A. D. O. Browere with me. Also, Browere's name does not appear in San Francisco City directories after 1852; Joan Hunt, "Alburtus Del Orient Browere" (Crocker Art Museum Archives, Sacramento, Calif., October 1984).

4. Reynolds, "The Life and Work of Alburtus Del Orient Browere," 29.

5. "Sign Painter Succeeds in Genre Field," *New York Sun,* 10 February 1940, p. 9.

6. See, for example, Charles Deas, *Long Jakes,* 1844 (The Manoogian Collection, Detroit), or Arthur F. Tait, *The Prairie Hunter—One Rubbed Out!* 1852 (Autry Museum of Western Heritage, Los Angeles).

7. Hunt, "Alburtus Del Orient Browere," citing *The Columbia Gazette,* 5 August 1854.

8. Everett Millard, telephone conversation with author, 17 March 1997.

9. Elizabeth Johns, *American Genre Painting: The Politics of Everyday Life* (New Haven, Conn.: Yale University Press, 1991), 91.

10. Jeanne Van Nostrand and Edith Coulter, *California Pictorial: A History in Contemporary Pictures, 1786 to 1859* (Berkeley and Los Angeles: University of California Press, 1948), 103; see also note 5 above.

11. Browere's California landscapes also include *Mountains and Falls, California,* 1852/62, in the collection of The Art Institute of Chicago, and *Prospector in the Foothills of the Sierra, California,* ca. 1855, at the Carnegie Museum of Art, Pittsburgh.

12. Reynolds, "The Landscapes of Alburtus Del Orient Browere," 8.

13. *Jamestown or D. O. Mills' Mill* is undated and was at one time attributed to Juan Buckingham Wandesforde. Although Browere depicted many mining sites near Jamestown, this composition is somewhat unusual for the artist. See Janice Driesbach, "Landmarks of Early California Painting: The Crocker Art Museum Exhibition," *California History* 71 (spring 1992): 29.

14. Van Nostrand and Coulter, *California Pictorial,* 156.

15. As there are no surviving sketchbooks or drawings from Browere's residency in California, the term "sketch" may refer to such a small oil painting; Reynolds, "The Landscapes of Alburtus Del Orient Browere," 12–13.

16. Sally Mills in Marc Simpson, Sally Mills, and Jennifer Saville, *The American Canvas: Paintings from the Collection of The Fine Arts Museums of San Francisco* (New York: Hudson Hills Press in association with The Fine Arts Museums of San Francisco, 1989), 80.

17. Ibid.

18. R. E. Mather and F. E. Boswell, *John David Borthwick: Artist of the Gold Rush* (Salt Lake City, Utah: University of Utah Press, 1989), 114; Reynolds, "The Life and Work of Alburtus Del Orient Browere," 28.

19. Reynolds, "The Landscapes of Alburtus Del Orient Browere," 14; Georgia Willis Read, "The Chagres River Route to California in 1851," *Quarterly of the California Historical Society* 8 (March 1929): 4.

20. Reynolds, "The Life and Work of Alburtus Del Orient Browere," 31.

21. Read, "The Chagres River Route," 4.

22. The association between Browere's paintings and earlier

examples by Cole is made in Diana Strazdes, *American Paintings and Sculpture to 1945* (New York: Hudson Hills Press in association with The Carnegie Museum of Art, 1992), 111. Browere could easily have seen Cole's *Voyage of Life* series when it was on exhibition in New York in 1840. Van Nostrand and Coulter (*California Pictorial,* 68) note that *Crossing the Isthmus* was originally owned by Theodore F. Payne of San Francisco.

23. Mather and Boswell, *John David Borthwick,* 79–80.

24. Hunt, "Alburtus Del Orient Browere."

25. Although the *Tuolumne Courier* of 16 March 1861 reported that Browere had "lately sold his 'Horse Picture' for $125 and the landscape, painted here, is now up for raffle," there is little additional information indicating that his paintings were in demand; Hunt, "Alburtus Del Orient Browere."

26. Reynolds, "The Landscapes of Alburtus Del Orient Browere," 12.

27. Ibid., 15.

28. Johns, *American Genre Painting,* 91.

IN THE WAKE OF THE GOLD RUSH

1. John S. Hittell, "Art in San Francisco," *Pacific Monthly* 10 (July 1863): 105.

2. Moreland L. Stevens, *Charles Christian Nahl: Artist of the Gold Rush, 1818–1878,* exh. cat. (Sacramento, Calif.: E. B. Crocker Art Gallery, 1976), 133–34.

3. *Daily Alta California* (San Francisco), 31 October 1859.

4. Ibid., 2 September 1860, p. 1; ibid., 29 December 1865, p. 1; Hittell, "Art in San Francisco," 105.

5. L. Eve Armentrout-Ma, "Chinese in California's Fishing Industry," *California History* 60 (summer 1981): 142.

6. Ibid.; also Robert F. G. Spier, "Food Habits of Nineteenth-Century California Chinese," *California Historical Society Quarterly* 37 (March 1958): 82.

7. *Report of the First Industrial Exhibition of the Mechanics' Institute of the City of San Francisco, September 7–26, 1857* (San Francisco, Calif.: Printed at the Franklin Office, 1858), 97.

8. *Frontier America: The Far West,* exh. cat. (Boston: Museum of Fine Arts, 1975), 126.

9. *Daily Alta California,* 11 September 1857.

10. *Report of the First Industrial Exhibition,* 101–102.

11. *Daily Alta California* (San Francisco), 3 September 1858; ibid., 8 September 1858; ibid., 9 September 1858.

12. Benjamin Parke Avery, "Art Beginnings on the Pacific," *Overland Monthly* 1 (August 1868): 116.

SENTIMENT AND NOSTALGIA

1. Edan Milton Hughes, *Artists in California, 1786–1940,* 2d ed. (San Francisco: Hughes, 1989), 3.

2. The Henry H. Clifford Collection of California Pictorial Letter Sheets, Dorothy Sloan—Rare Books (Austin, Texas) auction catalogue, 26 October 1994, lot 338.

3. Moreland L. Stevens, *Charles Christian Nahl: Artist of the Gold Rush, 1818–1878,* exh. cat. (Sacramento, Calif.: E. B. Crocker Art Gallery, 1976), 57.

4. J. D. Borthwick, *3 Years in California,* with index and foreword by Joseph A. Sullivan (Oakland, Calif.: Biobooks, 1948), 296.

5. Malcolm J. Rohrbough, *Days of Gold: The California Gold Rush and the American Nation* (Berkeley and Los Angeles: University of California Press, 1997), 138.

6. Joseph Armstrong Baird Jr., ed., *France and California* (Davis, Calif.: University of California, 1967), 16.

7. Ibid.

A watercolor study for this painting, 15 × 27½ in. (sight), is inscribed on its mat (at lower center): "San Francisco/Spring 1850/From the head of Clay Street/An original watercolor/by/Geo. H. Burgess/Made for James C. Flood" (collection, Society of California Pioneers, San Francisco).

8. Baird, *France and California,* p. 16.

9. Bret Harte, *The Luck of Roaring Camp and Other Sketches* (Boston: Houghton Mifflin, 1903), 14.

Selected Bibliography

Arkelian, Marjorie. *Tropical: Tropical Scenes by 19th Century Painters of California.* Exh. cat. Oakland, Calif.: The Oakland Museum, 1971.

———. *The Kahn Collection of Nineteenth-Century Paintings by Artists in California.* Exh. cat. Oakland, Calif.: The Oakland Museum, 1975.

Avery, Benjamin Parke. "Art Beginnings on the Pacific." *Overland Monthly* 1 (July 1868): 28–34; (August 1868): 113–18.

Ayres, William, ed. *Picturing History: American History Painting 1770–1930.* New York: Rizzoli International and Fraunces Tavern Museum, 1993.

Baird, Joseph Armstrong, Jr. "Catalogue of Original Paintings, Drawings and Watercolors in the Robert B. Honeyman, Jr. Collection." MS. The Bancroft Library, University of California, Berkeley, 1964-65.

Borthwick, John David. *Three Years in California.* Edinburgh: Blackwood, 1857.

California Centennial's Exhibition of Art. Exh. cat. Los Angeles: Los Angeles County Museum, 1949.

Caughey, John Walton, ed. "Life in California in 1849: As Described in the 'Journal' of George F. Kent." *California Historical Society Quarterly* 20 (March 1941): 26–46.

Delano, Alonzo. *Life on the Plains and Among the Diggings.* Auburn, N.Y.: Miller, Orton and Mulligan, 1854.

Driesbach, Janice T. "Landmarks of Early California Painting: The Crocker Art Museum Exhibition." *California History* 71 (spring 1992): 24–32.

Ewers, John C. *Artists of the Old West.* Garden City, N.Y.: Doubleday, 1965.

Gerdts, William H. *Art Across America: Two Centuries of Regional Painting,* Vol. 3. New York: Abbeville Press, 1990.

Hart, James T. *A Companion to California.* New York: Oxford University Press, 1978.

Haskins, C. W. *The Argonauts of California: Being the Reminiscences and Incidents That Occurred in California in Early Mining Days.* New York: Fords, Howard and Hulbert, 1890.

Hills, Patricia. *The American Frontier: Images and Myths.* Exh. cat. New York: Whitney Museum of American Art, 1973.

Hittell, John S. "Art in San Francisco." *Pacific Monthly* 10 (July 1863): 99–107.

Hughes, Edan Milton. *Artists in California, 1786–1940.* 2d ed. San Francisco: Hughes, 1989.

Johns, Elizabeth. *American Genre Painting: The Politics of Everyday Life.* New Haven, Conn.: Yale University Press, 1991.

Jurmain, Claudia K., and James J. Rawls, eds. *California: A Place, A People, A Dream.* San Francisco and Oakland, Calif.: Chronicle Books and The Oakland Museum, 1986.

Kirk, Anthony. "In a Golden Land So Far: The Rise of Art in Early California." *California History* 71 (spring 1992): 2–23.

Kowalewski, Michael. "Imagining the California Gold Rush: The Visual and Verbal Legacy." *California History* 71 (spring 1992): 60–73.

Lamson, Joseph. Diaries, letter-journals, January 1852 to October 1862, MS. Collection of the California Historical Society, San Francisco.

M. and M. Karolik Collection of American Water Colors & Drawings 1800–1875. Boston: Museum of Fine Arts, 1962.

McDermott, John Francis, ed. *An Artist on the Overland Trail: The 1849 Diary and Sketches of James F. Wilkins.* San Marino, Calif.: Huntington Library, 1967.

Mather, R. E., and F. E. Boswell. *John David Borthwick: Artist of the Gold Rush.* Salt Lake City, Utah: University of Utah Press, 1989.

Peters, Harry T. *California on Stone.* Garden City, N.Y.: Doubleday, Doran, 1935.

Report of the First Industrial Exhibition of the Mechanics' Institute of the City of San Francisco, September 7–26, 1857. San Francisco: Printed at the Franklin Office, 1858.

Rohrbough, Malcolm J. *Days of Gold: The California Gold Rush and the American Nation.* Berkeley and Los Angeles: University of California Press, 1997.

Severson, Thor. *Sacramento: An Illustrated History: 1839–1874 from Sutter's Fort to Capital City.* San Francisco: California Historical Society, 1973.

Soulé, Frank, John H. Gihon, M.D., and James Nisbet. *The Annals of San Francisco Together with the Continuation through 1855.* Compiled by Dorothy H. Huggins. Palo Alto, Calif.: Lewis Osborne, 1966.

Spinazze, Libera Martina, et al. *The Index of People, Ships, Immigration and Mining Companies Mentioned in C. W. Haskins' The Argonauts of California.* MS compiled under the direction of the Society for California Pioneers, 1975.

Stanger, Frank M., ed. *Off for California: The Letters, Log, and Sketches of William H. Dougal, Gold Rush Artist.* Oakland, Calif.: Biobooks, 1949.

Taylor, Bayard. *El Dorado, or Adventures in the Path of Empire.* Introduction by Robert Glass Cleland. New York: Knopf, 1949.

Truettner, William H., ed. *The West as America: Reinterpreting Images of the Frontier, 1820–1920.* Exh. cat. Washington, D.C.: Smithsonian Institution Press for the National Museum of American Art, 1991.

Van Nostrand, Jeanne. *San Francisco, 1806–1906 in Contemporary Paintings, Drawings and Watercolors.* San Francisco: Book Club of California, 1975.

———. *The First Hundred Years of Painting in California, 1775–1875.* San Francisco: John Howell-Books, 1980.

Van Nostrand, Jeanne, and Edith M. Coulter. *California Pictorial: A History in Contemporary Pictures, 1786 to 1859.* Berkeley and Los Angeles: University of California Press, 1948.

PHOTOGRAPHY CREDITS

Reproductions of the objects in the exhibition are made possible by permission of the lenders. Lending institutions supplied the color transparencies; additional photography credits follow:

Armen, page 46; Brooks Photo, page 59; William B. Dewey, page 53; M. Lee Fatherree, pages xviii, 6, 16, 21, 23, 25, 27, 34, 41, 42, 45, 48, 52, 57, 58, 60, 67, 68, 69, 71, 73, 76, 80, 82, 85, 89, 94, 95, 104, 115; Don Hagopian, page 12; Cecile Keefe, page 83; Scott McClaine, page 106; James O. Milmoe, page 89; R. G. Ojeda, page 13; Michael Tropea, page 78; Witt, page 87.

Artists Represented in the Exhibition

ARTIST UNKNOWN
A Lucky Striker (A.G.)
Mining Scene: Diverting a River
Mining in California

JOHN WOODHOUSE AUDUBON
Twenty-five Miles West of Jesus Maria
Murphy's New Diggings (Oak of the Hills)
Hawkin's Bar
Sacramento City
San Francisco

THOMAS A. AYRES
San Francisco Bay
Sunrise at Camp Lonely from the South, Looking North
Camp Lonely from the North . . . by Moonlight
Bay of San Francisco, View from Telegraph Hill Looking Toward Saucelito
North Beach: San Francisco from Off Meigs' Wharf

HENRY BACON
The Luck of Roaring Camp

ALBURTUS DEL ORIENT BROWERE
The Lone Prospector
Miner's Return
Miners of Placerville
Prospectors in the Sierra
Jamestown or D. O. Mills' Mill
View of Stockton
Mokelumne Hill
Crossing the Isthmus

GEORGE HENRY BURGESS
Hunters in the Gold Country
Untitled (man crossing a stream)
Miners Working Beside a Stream
Artist's Gold Mining Camp
Mining at Tunnel Hill, Jackson, Amador County, California
Mother Lode Inn
View of San Francisco in 1850

FREDERICK BUTMAN
Surveyor's Camp
Hunter's Point
Chinese Fishing Village

JOHN HENRY DUNNEL
Sutter's Mill at Coloma

HARRISON EASTMAN
Saint Francis Hotel, Cor. Clay and Dupont Sts.

ALEXANDER EDOUART
Blessing of the Enrequita Mine

AUGUSTO FERRAN
San Francisco: View from the Hills to Northwest
Vista de San Francisco

WASHINGTON F. FRIEND
Placer Mining

E. GODCHAUX
Vue de San-Francisco en 1851

WILLIAM SMITH JEWETT
Captain Washington A. Bartlett, U.S.N.
Hock Farm (A View of the Butte Mountains from Feather River, California)
Captain Ned Wakeman
Portrait of General John A. Sutter (1856)

WILLIAM McILVAINE
Panning Gold, California
Prairie, California

WILLIAM BIRCH McMURTRIE
View of Telegraph Hill and City, North on Montgomery Street

FRANCIS SAMUEL MARRYAT
San Francisco Fire of 17 September 1850

E. HALL MARTIN
Mountain Jack and a Wandering Miner
The Prospector

CHARLES CHRISTIAN NAHL
Chagres River Scene (Crossing the Chagres)
Boaters Rowing to Shore at Chagres
Little Miss San Francisco
Portrait of Jane Eliza Steen Johnson
Sunday Morning in the Mines
Dead Miner
Forest Burial

CHARLES CHRISTIAN NAHL and
HUGO WILHELM ARTHUR NAHL
The Camp of a U.S. Coast Geodetic Survey Party
Fire in San Francisco Bay

CHARLES CHRISTIAN NAHL and
FREDERICK AUGUST WENDEROTH
Miners in the Sierra

HUGO WILHELM ARTHUR NAHL
The Fire in Sacramento

ERNEST NARJOT
Placer Operations at Foster's Bar
The Forty-Niner
Miners: A Moment at Rest (Gold Rush Camp)
French Gold-Seekers in California

SAMUEL STILLMAN OSGOOD
General John A. Sutter

JOHN PRENDERGAST
San Francisco after Fire

W. TABER
Steam Gold Dredger Ascending the Sacramento

GEORGE TIRRELL
View of Sacramento, California, from Across the Sacramento River

FREDERICK AUGUST WENDEROTH
Portrait of a Man

RUFUS WRIGHT
The Card Players

Index

NOTE: Page numbers in *italics* indicate illustrations.

A

"A. G." (unknown), *A Lucky Striker,* 25, *25*
Album Californiano (Tipos Californianos), 12 Realizacion. Selling Off (Ferran), 17, *17*
allegory, in Gold Rush art, 11, 89, 104–105
Alta California (newspaper), 11, 38
  see also *Daily Alta California*
American Academy of Fine Arts (New York), 11
American Art Union (New York), 10, 11
American River, 1
Argonauts, 2, 4, 101, 108
artists
  collaboration among, 48–49, 51, 52–56, 59
  as a community, 5, 72–73, 98–99, 102
  services offered by, 47, 62, 89, 101
  unknown, 26–27
Artist's Gold Mining Camp (Burgess), 69, *69*
art union, in San Francisco, 99
A Scene in Montgomery Street in 1851 (Eastman), 121
Audubon, John Woodhouse, 28–33
  biography of, 117
  Hawkin's Bar, 30, *31*
  Murphy's New Diggings (Oak of the Hills), 30, *30*
  Sacramento City, 30, *31,* 96
  San Francisco, *32,* 33
  Twenty-five Miles West of Jesus Maria, 28, *29*
Avery, Benjamin Parke, 5
Ayres, Thomas A., 5, 7–10, 98, 101
  biography of, 117–18
  Bay of San Francisco, View from Telegraph Hill Looking Toward Saucelito, 8, *9*
  Camp Lonely from the North . . . by Moonlight, 7, *8*
  North Beach: San Francisco from Off Meigs' Wharf, 8, *9*
  San Francisco Bay, *6,* 7–8
  Sunrise at Camp Lonely from the South, Looking North, 7, *7*

B

Bacon, Henry
  biography of, 118
  The Luck of Roaring Camp, 112, *113,* 118
Bartlett, Washington A., *36,* 39
Baturone, José, 17
Bay of San Francisco, View from Telegraph Hill Looking Toward Saucelito (Ayres), 8, *9*
Beale, Edwin F., 1
Bierstadt, Albert, 5, 98, 102
Bigler, John, 43
Blessing of the Enrequita Mine (Edouart), 93, 96, *97*
Boaters Rowing to Shore at Chagres (C. C. Nahl), 57–58, *58*
Borneo and the Indian Archipelago (Marryat), 33, 125
Borthwick, John David, 65, 89, 105, 108
Boy Fishing (Martin), 11
Brannan, Samuel, 1, 110
Britton and Rey (lithographers), 72
Brookes, Samuel Marsden, 5, 98
Browere, A. D. O., 3, 77–90
  biography of, 118–19
  style of, 4
  Canonicus and the Governor of Plymouth, *77*
  Catskill, New York, 77, *77*
  Crossing the Isthmus, 87, *88*
  Goldminers, 4, 87, 89, *89*
  Jamestown or D. O. Mills' Mill, 82, *83*
  John C. Duchow, Jr., 80, *80*
  Miners of Placerville, 4, 80, *81*
  Miner's Return, *78,* 79–80
  Mokelumne Hill, 84, *86,* 87
  Prospectors in the Sierra, 80, *82*
  Rip Van Winkle, 77, *79*
  South of Tuolumne City, *89,* 90
  Stockton, 82, 84, *85*
  The Lone Prospector, 4, *76,* 79, 89
  The Trail of the '49ers, 87, *87*
  View of Stockton, 82, *85*
Burgess, Charles, 66, 72
Burgess, Edward, 66, 70
Burgess, George Henry, 66–75, 98, 102
  biography of, 119–20
  in Hawaii, 72
  lithography by, 72, 101
  as a portrait painter, 72
  Artist's Gold Mining Camp, 69, *69*
  Hunters in the Gold Country, 67, *67*
  Miners Working Beside a Stream, 68–69, *68*
  Mining at Tunnel Hill, Amador County, California, 70, *71*
  Mother Lode Inn, 70, *71*
  Port of Honolulu, 72
  San Francisco in July, 1849, 21, *73,* 74–75, 120
  Untitled (man crossing a stream), 67–68, *68*
  View of San Francisco in 1850, 73, 110, *111*

Burgess, Hubert, 66–67, 72, 98
Butman, Frederick A., 52, 91–93, 98
biography of, 120
Chinese Fishing Village, 93, 95
Hunter's Point, 93, 94
Surveyor's Camp, 52, 91, 92

C

California, routes to, 1–2, 4, 28, 56, 77, 87
California News (Mount), 2–3, *3*
California School of Design, 99, 102, 114
California Star, The (newspaper), 110
Camp Lonely from the North . . . by Moonlight (Ayres), 7, *8*
Camp of a U.S. Geodetic Survey Party, The (C. C. Nahl and Arthur Nahl), 52, *53,* 54, 56
Canonicus and the Governor of Plymouth (Browere), 77
Captain Ned Wakeman (Jewett), 42, *42*
Captain Washington A. Bartlett, U.S.N. (Jewett), *36,* 39–40
Card Players, The (Wright), 114, *115*
Castle of San Juan d'Ulloa (Martin), 11
Catskill, New York (Browere), 77, *77*
Century Magazine, 20
Chagres (Panama), 4, 56–58
Chagres River Scene (Crossing the Chagres) (C. C. Nahl), 56–57, *57*
chiaroscuro, 68
Chinese Fishing Village (Butman), 93, *95*
chromolithograph, 75
Claude Lorrain, 39, 40
Cogswell, William, 4
Cole, Thomas, *The Voyage of Life: Youth,* 87, *87*
collaboration, among artists, 48–49, 51, 52–56, 59
Coloma (California), 2, 39, 40, 120
Colonel Collier (Jewett), 40
Columbia (California), 79, 80, 89
Columbia Gazette (newspaper), 80
commissions, 38, 52, 73, 80, 91, 110
Cook, Elisha, 74
Cota de Temple, Rafaela, 44
Crocker, Judge Edwin Bryant, as a patron, 62–63, 103
Crossing the Isthmus (Browere), 87, *88*
Crossing the Plains (C. C. and A. Nahl), 48

D

daguerreotypes, 3, 48, 58, 62
Daily Alta California (newspaper), 40, 42, 98
see also *Alta California*
Davis, Solomon, 79
Dead Miner (C. C. Nahl), 102–103, *103*
Deas, Charles, 79
Delacroix, Eugène, 63
Denny, Gideon Jacques, 98
Duchow, John C. Jr., 80, *80*
Dunnel (Dunnell), John Henry, 98
biography of, 120
Sutter's Mill at Coloma, 25–26, *26*

E

Eastman, Harrison, 11, 21, 23, 98, 101
biography of, 121
A Scene in Montgomery Street in 1851, 121
Lombard, North Point and Greenwich Docks, San Francisco, 121
Miner's Ten Commandments, The, 121
Saint Francis Hotel, Cor. Clay and Dupont Sts., 4, 21, 23, *23*
Edouart, Alexander, 91, 93, 96, 98
biography of, 121
portraits by, 98
Blessing of the Enrequita Mine, 93, 96, 97
Eldridge family, 96
environment, effect of gold mining on, 68
exhibitions, of art, 91, 98–99, 101
in New York, 10
in San Francisco, 8, 72–73, 91
see also Mechanics' Institute

F

Fair
Ladies Christian Commission, 46, 99
State, art exhibitions at, 48, 101
Fandango (C. C. Nahl), 63, *63*
Feather River, 40, *41*
fees, for commissions, 37, 38, 43, 73, 74–75
Ferran, Augusto, 17
biography of, 121–22
Album Californiano (Tipos Californianos), 122
12. Realizacion. Selling Off, 17, *17*
San Francisco: View from the Hills to the Northwest, 18
Vista de San Francisco, 4, *18*
fire, prevalence of, 3–4, 15, 33, 39, 49, 52

Fire in Sacramento, The (Arthur Nahl), 52, *52*
Fire in San Francisco Bay (C. C. Nahl and A. Nahl), 54, *55*, *56*
Flood, James Clair, 73, 110
Forest Burial (C. C. Nahl, attrib.), *104*, 105
Forty-Niner, The (Narjot), 105, *106*, 108
Foster's Bar, *64*, 65
France, miners from, 87, 105, 108, 109
Frémont, John C., 120
French Gold-Seekers in California (Narjot), 66, 109, *109*
Friend, Washington F.
  biography of, 122
  Placer Mining, 26, *26*

G

General John A. Sutter (Osgood), 23, *24*, 25
genre. *See* painting, genre
Georgetown (California), 39
Géricault, Théodore, 63
Godchaux, E.
  biography of, 122
  Vue de San-Francisco en 1851, 33, *35*
gold, discovery of, 1
Goldminers (Browere), 4, 87, 89, *89*
gouache, 7
Grayson, Andrew Jackson, commission from, for Jewett, 38–39
Green Springs (California), 30
Greenwell, Captain W. E., 52, 91

H

Hangtown. *See* Placerville
Harper's Weekly, 10, 118
Harte, Bret, 110, 111, 114
Hawaii, 66, 72
Hawkin's Bar (Audubon), 30, *31*
Heilbron, Fred, 49
He Rastled with My Finger (Remington), 112
Hill, Thomas, 5, 98, 102
History of Napoleon (Laurent), 103
Hittell, John S., 5
Hock Farm (A View of the Butte Mountains from Feather River, California) (Jewett), 40, *41*
Hock Farm (Jewett), 40, *41*
Hotchkiss Hill (California), 39
Hunters in the Gold Country (Burgess), 67, *67*
Hunter's Point (Butman), 93, *94*
Hutchings, James Mason, 10, 118, 121

I

Illustrated California News, 11
Illustrated Notes of an Expedition through Mexico and California (Audubon), 117
Illustrated Placer Times and Transcript (newspaper), 47
Incident on the Chagres River (C. C.Nahl), 57
Ingres, Jean-August-Dominique, 63
  Madame Moitessier, 61, *61*
  Oedipus and the Sphinx, 13, *13*

J

Jack, Six-Fingered, 14
Jackson (California), 70, *71*
Jamestown or D. O. Mills' Mill (Browere), 82, *83*
J. E. Murdoch as Hamlet (Jewett), 44
Jewett, William Smith, 3, 37–46, 58, 91, 99
  biography of, 122–23
  landscape painting by, 40
  success of, 37, 42, 44, 46
  Captain Ned Wakeman, 42, *42*
  Captain Washington A. Bartlett, U.S.N., *36*, 39–40
  Colonel Collier, 40
  Hock Farm, 40, *41*
  Hock Farm (A View of the Butte Mountains from Feather River, California), 40, *41*
  J. E. Murdoch as Hamlet, 44
  Portrait of General John A. Sutter (1855), 25, 42–44, *43*
  Portrait of General John A. Sutter (1856), 25, 44, *45*
  Pursued, 46, *46*
  The Light of the Cross, 44
  The Promised Land—The Grayson Family, 4, 38–39, *39*, 44, 123
  Yosemite Falls, 44, 46, *46*
Joaquin Murietta (C. C.Nahl), 63
John C. Duchow, Jr. (Browere), 80, *80*
Johnson, Captain, 13
Johnson, Jane Eliza Steen, *60*, 61–62

K

Keith, William, 102
Kunath, Oscar, *The Luck of Roaring Camp*, 112, *112*

L
landscape, 40, 57–58, 90, 101–102
exhibitions of, 98
with figures, 80–89
idealized, 68, 93
mining sites and, 4
Laurent, Matthieu, 103
letter sheets, 73
Leutze, Emanuel, 80
Light of the Cross, The (Jewett), 44
lithography, 3, 17, *18*, 23, 48, 62, 72, 73, 103, 123
paintings for, 8, 40, 101
Little, John T., 39
Little Miss San Francisco (C. C. Nahl), 59, *59*, 61
Illustrated Place Times and Transcript (newspaper), 47
Lombard, North Point and Greenwich Docks, San Francisco (Eastman), Harrison, 121
Lone Prospector, The (Browere), 4, *76*, 79, 89
long tom. *See* sluice box
Love Chase, The (C. C.Nahl), 63
Luck of Roaring Camp, The (Bacon), 112, *113*, 118
Luck of Roaring Camp, The (Harte), 112
Luck of Roaring Camp, The (Kunath), 112, *112*
Lucky Striker, A ("A. G." [unknown]), 25, *25*

M
McIlvaine, William, 17, 20
biography of, 123–24
Panning Gold, California, 4, 17, *19*, 20, 26
Prairie, California, 4, 20, *20*
Sketches of Scenery and Notes of Personal Adventures in California and Mexico, 17, 123
McMurtrie, William Birch
biography of, 124
View of Telegraph Hill and City, North on Montgomery Street, 21, *22*, 74
Madame Moitessier (Ingres), 61, *61*
Marine View (Martin), 11
Marryat, Francis Samuel, 33, 42
biography of, 124–25
San Francisco Fire of 17 September 1850, 33, *34*
Marshall, James, 1, 2
Martin, E. Hall, 5, 7, 10–14
biography of, 125
Boy Fishing, 11
Castle of San Juan d'Ulloa, 11
Marine View, 11
Mountain Jack, 14
Martin, E. Hall (*continued*)
Mountain Jack and a Wandering Miner, *xviii*, 4, 10, 13–14
The Prospector, 10, *12*, 13
Wreck of the U.S. Brig Somers, 11
Marysville (California), 48
Mason, Richard, 1
Mechanic's Institute, 72, 91, 101, 103
First Industrial Exhibition, 5, 44, 93, 98, 120, 121, 123
Miner Prospecting, A (C. C. Nahl and August Wenderoth), 48, 79
Miners: A Moment at Rest (Gold Camp) (Narjot), *107*, 108–109
Miner's Cabin, Result of the Day (C.C. Nahl and August Wenderoth), 48, *49*
Miners of Placerville (Browere), 4, 80, *81*
Miner's Return (Browere), *78*, 79–80
Miners in the Sierra (C. C. Nahl and August Wenderoth), 17, 49, *50*, 51
Miner's Ten Commandments, The (Eastman), 121
Miners Working Beside a Stream (Burgess), 68–69, *68*
miniatures, 47, 48, *48*
mining, technology, 4, 17, 26–27, 51, 65, 70, 80
Mining at Tunnel Hill, Amador County, California (Burgess), 70, *71*
Mining in California, 27–28, *28*, 96
Mining Scene: Diverting a River, 26–27, *27*
Mokelumne Hill (Browere), 84, *86*, 87
Morse, Dr. John Frederick, 14
Mother Lode Inn (Burgess), 70, *71*
Mountain Jack (Martin), 14
Mountain Jack and a Wandering Miner (Martin), *xviii*, 4, 10, 13–14
Mountains and Molehills (Marryat), 33, 125
Mount, William Sidney, *California News*, 2–3, *3*
Murphy's New Diggings (Oak of the Hills) (Audubon), 30, *30*

N
Nahl, Laura, 51
Nahl, Charles Christian, 3, 42, 47–63, 91, 102
biography of, 125–26
and lithography, 23, 101
palette of, 56, 58, 63, 105
portraits by, 58–62, 98
themes of, 102
as a trained artist, 42
trilogy by, of Romans and the Sabine women, 63
Boaters Rowing to Shore at Chagres, 57–58, *58*
Chagres River Scene (Crossing the Chagres), 56–57, *57*

Nahl, Charles Christian (*continued*)
Dead Miner, 102–103, *103*
Fandango, 63, *63*
Forest Burial, *104,* 105
Incident on the Chagres River, 57
Joaquin Murietta, 63
Little Miss San Francisco, 59, *59,* 61
Portrait of Jane Eliza Steen Johnson, *60,* 61–62
Sunday in the California Diggings, 105
Sunday Morning in the Mines, cover, 63, *100,* 103–105
The Love Chase, 63
The Patriotic Race, 63
and Frederick August Wenderoth
A Miner Prospecting, 48, 79
Miner's Cabin, Result of the Day, 48, 49
Miners in the Sierra, 17, 49, *50,* 51
and Hugo Wilhelm Arthur Nahl
Crossing the Plains, 48
Fire in San Francisco Bay, 54, *55,* 56
Saturday Night at the Mines, 48–49, *49,* 105
The Camp of a U.S. Geodetic Survey Party, 52, *53,* 54, 56
Nahl, Hugo Wilhelm Arthur, 42, 47, 52, 59, 63, 91, 102, 121
biography of, 126–27
and lithography, 101
The Fire in Sacramento, 52, *52*
Narjot, Ernest, 65–66, 102, 105
biography of, 127
style of, 66, 109
French Gold-Seekers in California, 66, 109, *109*
Miners: A Moment at Rest (Gold Camp), 66, *107,* 108–109
Placer Operations at Foster's Bar, *64,* 65
The Forty-Niner, 66, 105, *106,* 108
National Academy of Design (New York), 77
Native Americans, as subjects, 8, 49, 65, 70
New Almaden (California), 27–28, 96, 97
North Beach: San Francisco from Off Meigs' Wharf (Ayres), 8, 9
nostalgia, for the Gold Rush, 102, 105, 108, 109, 110

O

Oedipus and the Sphinx (Ingres), 13, *13*
Osgood, Samuel Stillman, 24
biography of, 127–28
General John A. Sutter, 23, *24,* 25
Overland Monthly, The (periodical), 112

P

painting
Düsseldorf school, 80
genre, 54, 104–106
about mining, 4, 101, 109
by Charles Christian Nahl, 56
by Narjot, 66
history, 54, 56, 74, 110
Hudson River school, 40, 77, 84
Panama, depictions of, 4, 56–58, 87, *87, 88*
Panning Gold, California (McIlvaine), 4, 17, *19,* 20, 26
panorama, of western landscapes, 8, 38, 52
Panorama of California (Tirrell), 128, 129
Parisian Art and Artists (Bacon), 118
Parisian Year, A (Bacon), 118
Patriotic Race, The (C. C. Nahl), 63
patronage, 5, 80, 89, 91–92
and preferences for European art, 62, 114
see also commissions
photography, 96
hand-painting, 72
see also daguerreotypes
Placer Mining (Friend)
Placer Operations at Foster's Bar (Narjot), *64,* 65
Placerville (Hangtown), 80, *81*
Plain Language from Truthful James (The Heathen Chinee) (Harte), 114
Polk, James K., 1
population, 2, 73
Port of Honolulu (Burgess), 72
Portrait of General John A. Sutter (1855) (Jewett), 25, 42–44, *43*
Portrait of General John A. Sutter (1856) (Jewett), 25, 44, *45*
Portrait of Jane Eliza Steen Johnson (C. C. Nahl), *60,* 61–62
Portrait of a Man (Wenderoth), 48, *48*
portraiture, 5, 22, 98
see also Jewett, William Smith; Nahl, Charles Christian
Poussin, Nicolas, 63
Prairie, California (McIlvaine), 4, 20, *20*
Prendergast, John, 15, 110
biography of, 128
San Francisco after Fire, 15, *16*
prints, from the Gold Rush, 23, 40
Promised Land, The—The Grayson Family (Jewett), 4, 38–39, *39,* 44, 123
Prospectors in the Sierra (Browere), 80, *82*
Prospector, The (Martin), 10, *12,* 13
Pursued (Jewett), 46, *46*

Q
quicksilver mining, 27–28, *28*, 96, 97

R
Remington, Federic, *He Rastled with My Finger,* 112
Reynolds, A., 13
Rip Van Winkle (Browere), 77, 79
Rix, Julian, 102
Rough and Ready (Calfornia), 47, 49
Ryan, William Redmond

S
Sacramento (California), 1, 11
depictions of, *31,* 33, 52, *52,* 96, 98, 99
Sacramento City (Audubon), *31,* 33, 96
Sacramento Daily Bee (newspaper), 43
Sacramento River, 21
Sacramento Union (newspaper), 14
Saint Francis Hotel, Cor. Clay and Dupont Sts. (Eastman), 4, 21, 23, *23*
San Francisco: View from the Hills to the Northwest (Ferran), *18*
San Francisco
as an art center, 101, 110
depictions of, 8, *9,* 15–*16,* 17, *18,* 21–*23,* *32,* 33, 54, *55,* *73,* 74, 110, *111,* 129
growth of, 8, 21, *22,* 73–74
San Francisco after Fire (Prendergast), 15, *16*
San Francisco Art Association, 73, 99, 102, 114
San Francisco (Audubon), *32,* 33
San Francisco Bay (Ayres), *6,* 7–8
San Francisco Fire of 17 September 1850 (Marryat), 33, *34*
San Francisco in July, 1849 (Burgess), 21, *73,* 74–75, 120
San Joaquin River, 82
Sarony and Major (lithographers), 40
Sartain, John, 25
Saturday Night at the Mines (C. C. and A. Nahl), 48–49, *49,* 105
Sketches of Scenery and Notes of Personal Adventures in California and Mexico (McIlvaine), 17, 123
sluice box (long tom), 26, *26,* *50,* 51
Smith, Thomas A., 8
Sonora (California), 20, 66
South of Tuolumne City (Browere), *89,* 90
speaking trumpet, 41
Steam Gold Dredger Ascending the Sacramento (Taber), 20–21, *21*
Stevenson, Colonel Jonathan D., 66
Stockton (Browere), 82, 84, *85*
Stockton (California), 82, 84
Sunday in the California Diggings (C. C. Nahl), 105
Sunday Morning in the Mines (C. C. Nahl), *cover,* 63, *100,* 103–105
Sunrise at Camp Lonely from the South, Looking North (Ayres), 7, *7*
Surveyor's Camp (Butman), 91, *92*
Sutter, John, 1, 2, *24,* 25, 40, 43, *43,* *45*
Sutter's Fort, 1, 43, *43*
Sutter's Mill, *26,* 40, 120, 123
Sutter's Mill at Coloma (Dunnel), 25–26, *26*

T
Taber, W.
biography of, 128
Steam Gold Dredger Ascending the Sacramento, 20–21, *21*
Tait, W. F., 79
Temple, Don Juan, 44
Tipos Californianos. See *Album Californiano*
Tirrell, George, 91, 96, 98
biography of, 128–29
Panorama of California, 128, 129
View of Sacramento, California, from Across the Sacramento River, 96, 98, 99
Trail of the '49ers, The (Browere), 87, *87*
Treaty of Guadalupe Hidalgo, 1
trilogy
Martin's Forty-niner, 11–14
Nahl's Romans and the Sabine women, 63
triptych, McMurtrie's, 74
Tuolumne Courier (newspaper), 89
Twain, Mark, 42
Twenty-five Miles West of Jesus Maria (Audubon), 28, *29*

U
Untitled (man crossing a stream) (Burgess), 67–68, *68*

V
Vernet, Horace, 54, 103
View of Sacramento, California, from Across the Sacramento River (Tirrell), 96, 98, 99
View of San Francisco in 1850 (Burgess), 73, 110, *111*
View of Stockton (Browere), 82, *85*
View of Telegraph Hill and City, North on Montgomery Street (McMurtrie), 21, *22,* 74
Vista de San Francisco (Ferran), 4, *18*
Voyage of Life, The: Youth (Cole), 87, *87*
Vue de San-Francisco en 1851 (Godchaux), 33, *35*

W
Wandesford, Juan Buckingham, 102
War, Mexican, 66
watercolor, *68*, 70
  en grisaille, 52
  on ivory, 48
  see also gouache
Watkins, Commodore James Thomas, 44
Webb, Colonel Henry L., 28, 117
Wenderoth, Frederick August, 42, 47, 51, 98
  biography of, 129
  Portrait of a Man, 48, *48*
Williams, Virgil, 5, 102
Winter in the Mines (poem), 102
Wool, General, 43
Wreck of the U.S. Brig Somers (Martin), 11
Wright, Rufus
  biography of, 129–30
  The Card Players, 114, *115*

X
xenophobia, in the gold fields, 114

Y
Yosemite Falls (Jewett), 44, 46, *46*
Yosemite Valley, artists in, 10, 44, *46*, 91, 101, 118